THE ANXIETY TOOLKIT FOR TEENS

Easy and practical CBT and DBT tools
to manage your stress, anxiety, worry
and panic

A FREE GIFT FOR OUR READERS

A set of printable journals for teens including

ANXIETY JOURNAL

GRATITUDE JOURNAL

MINDFULNESS JOURNAL

Simply scan the QR code or go to
www.teen-thrive.com/printables

FOREWORD

Does it ever seem like everyone else has life figured out better than you do? Maybe other people seem to get better grades, study less, get more sleep, or have more friends, and do it all with ease, while you're feeling stressed and anxious. A lot of the teens I work with tell me they feel this way – like there's something wrong with them that will prevent them from having a happy or successful life, and that their stress or anxiety are proof of that. What these teens may not realize is just how common these feelings are. Nearly 1 in 3 teens has significant anxiety, and that number keeps growing.

Still other teens tell me that everyone they know is stressed or anxious and they don't think there's anything that can be done to make it better, so they don't want to bother wasting their time or energy on trying. They might either try to be super-human and push through or turn to unhealthy strategies that can cause more problems for them in the future. While these teens do have a point – stress and anxiety are emotions that everyone experiences at some point – what they may not realize is just how many great tools there are to help people deal with stress and anxiety in healthy ways that will make them feel more capable and give them more energy.

The pressures that teens face today are more than they were in the past. Pressure to be involved in tons of activities and do well at everything, to get into a "good" college, to be constantly connected and available to everyone, but to never say or do the wrong thing. It's hard to keep up with, and the stakes for every move you make can feel really high...like one wrong move could ruin your whole future. It makes sense that you would feel stressed or anxious in this situation, so it's no wonder that anxiety is such a common problem.

Even though anxiety is common, it's very treatable. But treatment doesn't mean getting rid of anxiety. It means learning to live with it without letting it take control and get in the way of enjoying your life. One of the things I love about this book is how useful it can be to every teen -- even if you don't have a diagnosis of an anxiety disorder. If you think anxiety is a sign there is something wrong with you, the explanations of anxiety in this book will show you just how normal and common, and necessary, anxiety is in our lives. If you don't think there's anything that can be done, it provides instructions for many different tools that have been proven to help manage anxiety and are easy to try.

This is also one of the most teen-friendly anxiety books I've seen. Self-help books can feel overwhelming, boring, or like a lot of work to use. This book is different. It packs a lot of useful information into an easy-to-read format that's fun and engaging, and provides exactly what it says it will – a toolkit to understand and manage anxiety, worry and stress. The tools for managing anxiety are divided into four categories – physical, thought, emotion, and behavior – with tips about what types of situations each tool may help with to make it easier for you to decide which tool to try at any given time. There's also a section with tips for what to say—and not say—when the people you care about are feeling anxious.

Whether you're a teen who wants to learn ways to handle anxiety on your own, a teen who works with a therapist and wants to add more to what you're learning in sessions, a parent who wants to understand your teen's anxiety better, or a therapist looking for resources to recommend to teens that they'll actually enjoy using, this toolkit is for you.

Ehrin Weiss, Ph.D.

Ehrin E Weiss, PhD

Psychologist
Houston Family Psychology, PLLC
Author of Anxiety Relief Book for Kids

TABLE OF CONTENTS

INTRODUCTION

Grades, scholarships, and student loans.
Failure, exclusion, and loneliness.
The decisions we need to make.
The chores we need to complete.
The older we get, the more they increase.

And let's be honest, the tradition carries on for the rest of our lives,
right up until we add bills and insurance to that list.

As a teenager, you probably already have quite a bit on your plate.

Classes and projects at school, try-outs for clubs and teams, thinking
about college or figuring out what you want to do with your life;

Navigating relationships at school or dealing with family at home;

Rediscovering your own body as it changes and grows;

And figuring out who you are and what your place is in the world.

You're not alone. Everyone makes the journey, and along that journey,
we all encounter stress or anxiety.

Some of us struggle a little more than the rest, while others may bump
into it much later in life.

In moments of anxiety, we may look around and ask ourselves,

Is anybody else anxious?

Am I the only one who is?

Is this normal?

Is something wrong with me?

Anxiety can be a lonely and frightening experience if you don't know what is happening. Learning about anxiety is the first step you can take to address it.

It can get overwhelming to learn about anxiety.

About 2,500,000,000 results (0.64 seconds)

There are about two billion five hundred million search results on Google for 'anxiety.'

So many people are talking about it, and many have different things to say. Some results offer scientific explanations; some are real-life experiences, and many are tools and hacks to deal with anxiety.

It can be challenging to filter out unnecessary information - unscientific explanations, misinformation, and unverified tools.

All the information in this toolkit is vetted by an expert, including the fifty tools to help you deal with different types of anxieties and situations.

HOW TO USE THIS TOOLKIT

This toolkit has fifty tools to deal with anxiety, stress, worry, and panic attacks. They are divided into four categories:

PHYSICAL TOOLS
Use your body

THOUGHT TOOLS
Use your mind

EMOTION TOOLS
Build your resistance

BEHAVIOR TOOLS
Habit management skills

Some tools may work better for you than others. You may use a combination of two tools. Experiment with the tools, see what works for you and what doesn't. You can tweak the tool to make it easier for you to do.

We have gathered these tools from different reliable sources: psychotherapies like Cognitive Behavioral Therapy (CBT), Dialectical Behavior Therapy (DBT) and Acceptance and Commitment Therapy (ACT); as well as books by influential people, like Dwight Eisenhower, the 34th US President.

And all of this, available in less than 200 pages. So, let's get started by understanding what anxiety is.

CHAPTER 1
THE ANXIETY SQUAD

Anxiety is a part of The Anxiety Squad, a band of emotions whose duty is to protect us.

There are five members in the anxiety squad:

FEAR	WORRY	STRESS	ANXIETY	PANIC

The Guardian	The Thinker	The Strategist	The Spy	The Warrior

They have been around for ages, helping our species survive.

Each emotion has its own purpose, and in this chapter, we will learn how The Anxiety Squad protects us.

Let's begin by meeting them one by one. Remember that we are learning about emotions, which might differ from how you may otherwise use these words.

FEAR,
THE GUARDIAN

Fear, The guardian,
appears when something
in our environment signals
the brain that danger is upon
us. This could be an aggressive
animal, a loud explosion, or the
darkness of the night.

We suddenly feel an odd sensation in
our chest or stomach. Our hearts may
start to beat faster, and we may even feel
out of breath.

The source of the fear, also known as a
trigger, is generally known. For example, in
the case of an aggressive animal, we fear the
fatality it may cause us. Another essential
characteristic of fear is that it lingers as long
as the trigger* is around.

The role of fear is to make you pay attention
to what is causing you harm, so you can then
address it and keep yourself safe.

*Trigger - a term that describes a situation,
person, place, or object that causes any of
the emotions in The Anxiety Squad.

Worry, The Thinker aims to protect you like fear when the trigger is vague or yet to present itself. We are likely to worry about exam results, running out of money, or the safety of a loved one.

We may constantly think of the trigger cooking up responses to "what-if" questions in our heads. The role of worry is to problem-solve a situation before it occurs.

WORRY, THE THINKER

Our prehistoric ancestors had a lot of time on their hands after the sun went down. This time would go into preparing themselves for situations that they may come across in the future:

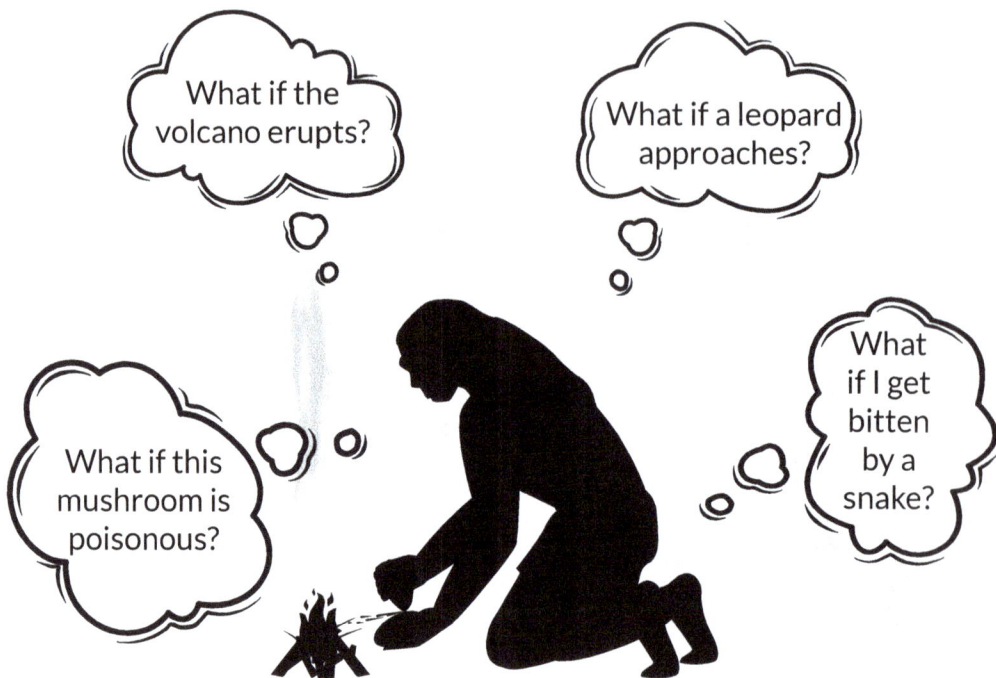

What if the volcano erupts?

What if a leopard approaches?

What if this mushroom is poisonous?

What if I get bitten by a snake?

Today, we don't need to worry about many of these things. We don't live in jungles anymore, and we have so much information at our fingertips. We could just look up the mushroom online and determine whether it is poisonous or not.

However, easy access to information can also contribute to worry in some cases. A typical example is looking up symptoms on the internet. You feel pain in your chest and look up "chest pain." The results include everything from heartburn to a heart attack, which can cause you to unnecessarily worry about your health.

STRESS,
THE STRATEGIST

Stress, The Strategist arrives when we are faced with a challenging situation. The trigger could be physical, like an illness or pain resulting from an injury, or mental, like a financial crisis or moving to a new city.

Our ancestors hunted and gathered, living on a day-to-day basis. Their sources of stress were likely venomous snakes, hungry leopards, and thieving monkeys. When the source of stress disappeared, so did the feeling of stress.

However, today's sources of stress are very different. They are situations that either last over a period of time (like an overwhelming schedule during exams) or things that are a daily part of our lives (traffic jams). These aren't sources that can be done away with by placing traps or building fences. They are sources that we regularly encounter that have to be dealt with repeatedly.

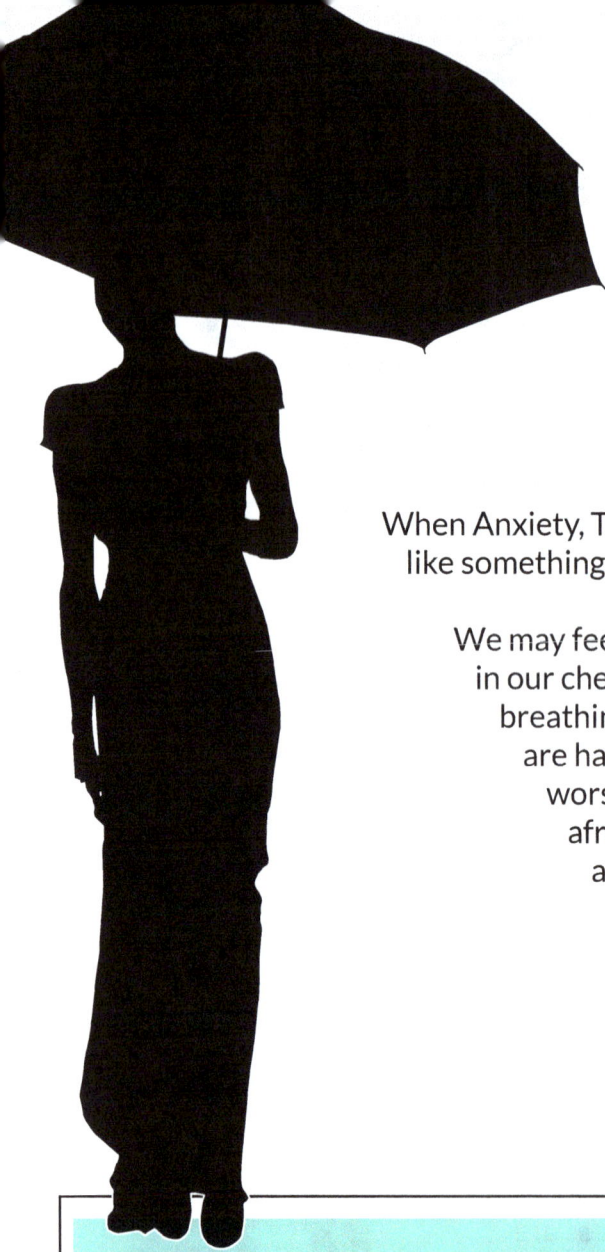

When Anxiety, The Spy, comes along, we feel like something terrible is going to happen.

We may feel shaky in the legs or tightness in our chest. We may be sweaty, and our breathing may quicken. Our thoughts are having a marathon, cooking up worst-case scenarios. We feel afraid, nervous, uncertain, tense, and restless.

ANXIETY,
THE SPY

The Spy is on the lookout for something that is about to harm us, but we don't know what.

The reason may be vague or perceived. A perceived threat is something that we define as a threat. This could be a life-threatening situation like encountering a bear in the woods. But it can also be something safe, like taking a flight.

Our perception is subjective and unique to us. Something that makes one person anxious may not necessarily have the same effect on another person.

A dancer may thrive on stage but be afraid to cross the street.

A pilot may take to the skies but have severe stage fright.

Some situations are nerve-racking for most people, like

An exam	A job interview	A public performance	A test result

PANIC,
THE WARRIOR

Panic, The Warrior, appears in cases where The Spy does not suffice. It is an extreme form of anxiety, like turning the dial to maximum. It's when you feel absolutely terrified and have a sense of impending doom.

We all experience moments of panic, but they last only a few seconds. This could be when we mistakenly think we have left our phone on the bus or missed the deadline for a project. Once we realize the mistake, we heave a sigh of relief and carry on.

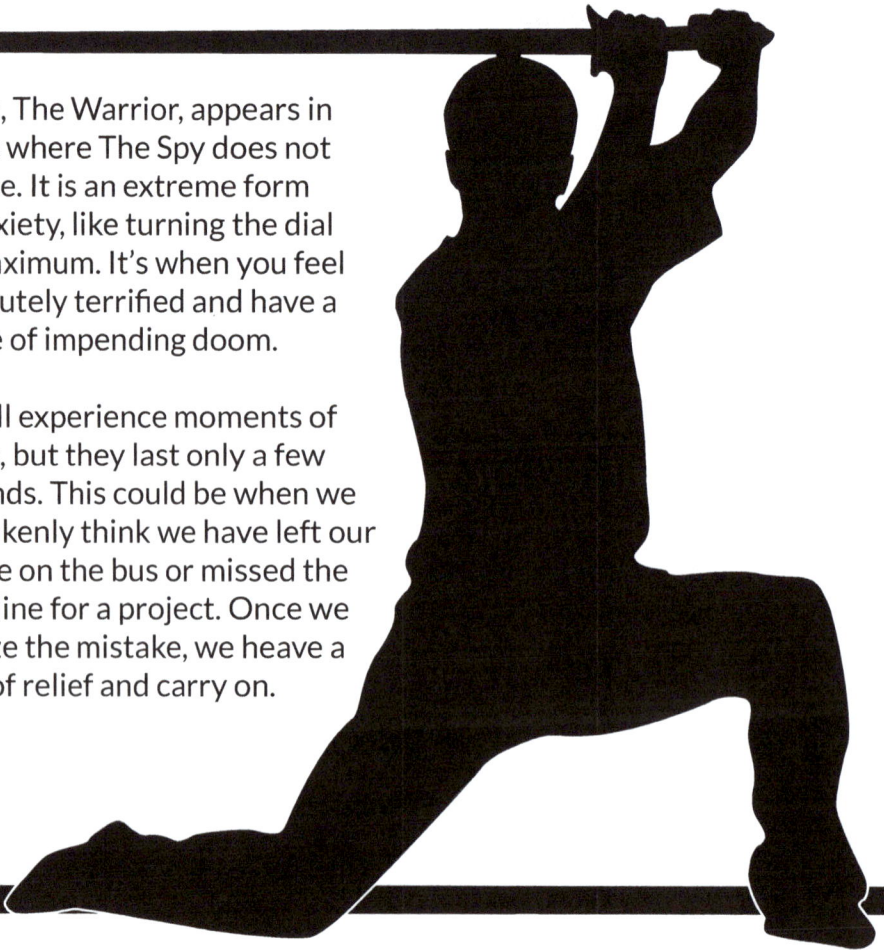

However, sometimes we may have a panic attack, a period of heightened anxiety. It is like a combination of fear and anxiety - as intense as fear, but the trigger is often vague or perceived like anxiety.

A panic attack can be confused with a serious health problem because of the chest pain or breathlessness that accompanies it. This can aggravate the attack by causing more stress and keeping us in a state of panic.

This is why it is essential to familiarize ourselves with The Anxiety Squad before dealing with them.

CHAPTER 2
THE ORIGIN STORY

THE

FFF

IGHT LIGHT REEZE

RESPONSE

The origin of The Anxiety Squad is a survival mechanism called the **fight-flight-freeze (FFF) response**. It is activated when the brain senses danger and is not limited to human beings. Can you identify what type of action (fight, flight, or freeze) the response triggered? (Answers are at the bottom)

1 A deer sees a leopard lurking in the bushes. The FFF response is activated instantly, sending the deer leaping in the other direction.

2 A monkey falls into a raging river and thrashes around for anything that can help it get to shore.

3 An octopus senses an unknown figure approaching and camouflages itself with the ocean floor.

4 A buffalo is standing its ground against a lion threatening its herd.

5 A possum plays dead and goes limp when it senses a human approaching.

Answers: 1. Flight 2. Fight 3. Freeze 4. Fight 5. Freeze

It is important to remember that not all danger is in the form of an opponent. For example, the monkey isn't faced by an actual predator that it must fight, but a situation it needs to fight itself out of.

Similarly, freezing can mean different reactions:

Playing dead: Pretending to be dead, like the possum.

Hiding: Taking cover until the danger has passed.

Appeasing: Co-operating instead of fighting to stay safe. For example, during a mugging.

Dissociation: Switching off mentally and going on 'autopilot' as the situation is too painful. For example, during trauma. This is also why victims may find it hard to recall specific details about traumatic incidents.

Depression: If the stressful event is continuous and overwhelming, it can lead to depression, which causes numbness, helplessness, and the feeling of being 'drained' of power.

WHAT HAPPENS DURING THE FFF RESPONSE?

The brain constantly receives information from our sensory organs: the eyes, nose, ears, skin, and tongue.

This information helps the brain to decide what to do and send signals to the body to execute the decisions.

For example, you feel raindrops on your skin. The brain registers that it's raining and that you need to find shelter to stay dry. It then sends signals to your eyes to find shelter and to your limbs to get you there.

It's raining!

On it.

When the brain receives information signaling danger, it activates the FFF response, releasing stress hormones like cortisol and adrenaline. A series of physiological changes are then triggered to help the brain make quick decisions and enable the body to execute them swiftly.

Every physiological change has a purpose. Here's a list of changes. Can you find the matching purpose for each?

	PHYSIOLOGICAL CHANGE		PURPOSE
1	Lung function increases	A	Better focus
2	Digestive system slows down or stops	B	Prevents excessive blood flow in case of injury
3	Pupils dilate	C	Makes the body swift and agile
4	Blood clotting function increases	D	Sends oxygen to the brain for faster decision making
5	Muscle tension increases	E	Provides body with extra energy
6	Blood pressure and blood sugar increase	F	Diverts blood to other areas

Answers: 1D. 2F. 3A. 4B. 5C. 6E.

Here's a complete list of the changes when the fight-or-flight response is activated.

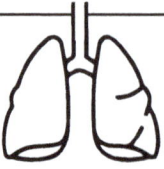

LUNG AND HEART FUNCTIONS INCREASE

WHY?

More oxygen reaches the brain, which helps it:

- Register more sensations
- Make quicker decisions
- Send signals faster

WHAT DOES IT FEEL LIKE?

- Your heart starts to race
- Blood rushes to your head
- Breathing becomes shallow and faster
- You may hyperventilate

DIGESTIVE SYSTEM SLOWS DOWN OR STOPS

BLADDER AND SPHINCTER MUSCLES RELAX

WHY?

- Diverts blood flow to other areas
- Prevents distractions like hunger or the need to use the loo

WHAT DOES IT FEEL LIKE?

- Loss of appetite
- Nausea/vomiting
- Instant urination or excretion

PUPILS DILATE

PERIPHERAL VISION REDUCES

WHY?

Better eyesight and focus to be alert to any changes in the situation

WHAT DOES IT FEEL LIKE?

- Alertness
- Sensitivity
- Vigilance

BLOOD PRESSURE AND BLOOD SUGAR INCREASE

BLOOD CLOTTING FUNCTION INCREASES

WHY?

- Offers the body an extra boost of energy
- Prevents excess blood flow in case of an injury

WHAT DOES IT FEEL LIKE?

- Sudden burst of energy
- Trembling
- Restlessness

MUSCLE TENSION INCREASES

BLOOD FLOW IS DIVERTED TOWARDS THE MUSCLES

WHY?

- Increases agility
- Blood flow carries oxygen and other minerals to muscles and increases stamina

WHAT DOES IT FEEL LIKE?

- Pins and needles
- Sweating
- Tingling or numbness

BRAIN FOCUSES ALL THOUGHTS ON THE SITUATION

WHY?

- Helps maintain focus
- Prevents distractions
- Sends new information

WHAT DOES IT FEEL LIKE?

- Racing thoughts
- Inability to focus on anything else

Once the danger passes, the brain signals the response to be turned off, and the body returns to normal.

The emotions of The Anxiety Squad are different ways in which our body responds to difficulty. Which member arrives to defend us depends on the threat.

If the danger is a bear in the woods, it can trigger Fear (The Guardian) or Panic (The Warrior) - which can help us make a quick escape.

A milder threat like loud thunder may warrant a weaker response, a rookie Spy like Anxiety, so we are vigilant for a storm.

We owe our lives to the FFF response. There would be no you and me, no man on the moon, and no anxiety toolkit without it. But, there is a downside.

Remember when we talked about Stress, The Strategist, that visits during overwhelming schedules and traffic jams? These situations can cause the brain to turn the response on and off several times, sometimes multiple times a day.

This means our body is producing stress hormones (cortisol and adrenaline) regularly and hyping up the different systems in our body by triggering physiological changes.

Over time, this can exhaust the brain and body. Going through the stress response often can affect our concentration and focus. It can also reduce our immunity and put us at risk of illness.

WHAT CAN TRIGGER THE FFF RESPONSE?

Anything.

Contrary to popular belief, The Anxiety Squad is not triggered by something that is inherently scary or worrying. It is triggered by the perception of a threat, meaning what the brain senses as danger.

This is what makes any of these emotions such a unique experience. Something that scares one person need not necessarily scare the other person.

It is also why we may "feel anxious for no reason." In these situations, the brain has categorized something as 'danger', but we aren't consciously aware of what that is.

Depending on the perception of the threat, the response can trigger any of the emotions from the Anxiety Squad.

Worry	Stressed out (Constant worry)	Anxiety	Panic

If you notice, we haven't included fear in the scale above. There is a difference between fear and the rest - the trigger. Let's look at two situations:

An aggressive animal

A public performance

In the first situation, we know exactly what we're afraid of - being attacked by the animal and having a fatal experience.

In the second situation, we're afraid of going on stage and being under the spotlight. But we may not know precisely why. We may fear embarrassment or that we're going to faint. But, there isn't a specific outcome that we're afraid of.

The other emotions are like the second situation. We aren't sure why we're anxious, what we're worried about exactly and why we are stressed out or panicking. It feels like a fear that comes out of nowhere.

CHAPTER 3
ANXIETY DISORDERS

The Anxiety Squad is a necessary feature, and like other essential features, it can malfunction.

In the same way that one can have diabetes from a malfunctioning pancreas, a person may experience issues with anxiety from a malfunctioning FFF response:

- The response getting activated for something that isn't a threat
- The response being activated more often than necessary
- The reaction being stronger than necessary

It is natural to be visited by The Anxiety Squad during a stressful time, like moving to a new city or in those isolated moments of panic.

However, an anxiety disorder is when the squad begins to interfere with your day-to-day life.

Anxiety disorders are categorized according to the nature of the triggers. Here are the most common anxiety disorders:

TRIGGER	ANXIETY DISORDER
Something specific	A phobia
Social interactions	Social anxiety
Life in general	Generalized-anxiety disorder
Anxiety and panic	Panic disorder
Reminders of a past event	Post-traumatic stress disorder

Let's look at them in more detail.

A phobia is an intense fear caused by the sight or thought of a particular thing, activity, situation, or person.

PHOBIA

For example, arachnophobia is the fear of spiders.

In the presence of a spider, it can cause thoughts like:

Something terrible is going to happen.

I'm going to die from fear.

The spider is going to kill/eat me.

I'm going to faint.

I'm having a heart attack.

I'm going to die.

I'm losing control.

The arachnophobia also affects behavior:

IN THE PRESENCE OF A SPIDER	IN DAILY LIFE
■ Freezing ■ Running away ■ Fainting ■ Crying or screaming ■ Feeling panicky	■ Avoiding spiders completely ■ Avoiding activities (like hiking and camping) where there may be spiders ■ Avoiding images and movies that mention or portray spiders

Many people are afraid of spiders. However, someone with arachnophobia cannot stand to be around a spider under any circumstances.

Even the tiniest spider in the world, which is the size of the head of a pin, can cause a panic attack.

◄———— SPIDER

For a fear to be diagnosed as a phobia, it has to be **intense**, **irrational**, and **incessant**.

Arachnophobia may not be very disrupting. It is possible to live peacefully in an urban setting, where it's easier to avoid spiders.

However, people may have a phobia of something that they have to deal with regularly, and this can cause complications in their lives:

- **Closed spaces** - avoiding taking an elevator or the subway
- **Dogs** - avoiding friends who have dogs
- **Flying** - skipping opportunities because it requires taking a flight
- **Dentists** - avoiding treatment, which makes the situation worse

People can opt for treatment and learn to manage their phobias in such cases.

There isn't a set construct of rules that defines a phobia. Some people may have a panic attack, while others may freeze. Every individual's experience of anxiety is distinct.

WHAT DO YOU FEAR IF YOU HAVE THESE PHOBIAS?

- Aerophobia
- Odontophobia
- Hemophobia
- Hypnophobia
- Numerophobia

- Pharmacophobia
- Pyrophobia
- Philophobia
- Hypochondria
- Cyberphobia

Note: You may come across words like homophobia, xenophobia, and islamophobia. These words do not suggest extreme fear. They are used to describe dislike or prejudice and are not the types of phobias that we're talking about.

Answers: Aerophobia - Flying, Odontophobia - Dentists, Hemophobia - Blood, Hypnophobia - Sleep, Numerophobia - Numbers, Pharmacophobia - Medicines, Pyrophobia - Fire, Philophobia - Love, Hypochondria - Illness, Cyberphobia - Computers.

Social anxiety is a disorder characterized by a fear of partaking in any kind of social interaction.

Social anxiety stems from the fear of judgment and can occur in situations like:

- Being introduced to someone new
- Being criticized in front of someone
- Being put in the spotlight
- Being observed while doing something
- Meeting people of authority, like the principal or an employer
- Speaking on the phone with a customer service representative
- Having to place an order at a restaurant
- Talking to a service provider, like a cashier or a bus driver

Let's explore the first situation: **being introduced to someone new**.

Imagine a gathering where there could be many people you don't know. Meeting someone new can be uncomfortable for most people. However, in the case of social anxiety, it can cause thoughts like:

They think I'm a loser.

They can read my mind.

They're going to laugh at me.

This is a prank of some kind.

I should leave before I embarrass myself.

Nobody wants me here.

What am I doing here? I don't belong here.

Am I standing properly?

I should have just stayed at home.

Please don't come and talk to me.

The social anxiety also affects behavior:

AT THE GATHERING, YOU MAY	IN DAILY LIFE, YOU MAY
- Have rigid body posture and movement - Avoid eye contact - Speak softly - Over-analyze others' expressions and body language - Sit on your own hands or keep them in your pocket to prevent trembling - Avoid conversations with new people and stick to people you know - Stay in the least crowded area - Avoid engaging in games or anything that puts you under the spotlight - Count the minutes until you can leave	- Cancel plans at the last minute or not show up - Make excuses not to go out - Go out for errands at odd times, so you don't run into other people - Be chatty on text but clam up in person - Avoid speaking on the phone - Prefer working alone instead of being in a team - Be on your phone around other people to avoid having conversations

Social anxiety should not be confused with introversion or shyness. While introverts may exhibit some of these traits, they aren't due to anxiety or fear of judgment.

Since social interactions appear in many aspects of our lives, social anxiety can cause significant disturbance to daily life.

Remember that any of these conditions can occur at different degrees. Someone may experience social anxiety only at work. Some may be okay with talking to service providers but become anxious while meeting new people.

Generalized-anxiety disorder (GAD) is an anxiety disorder that causes persistent feelings of anxiety that are either disproportional or unwarranted.

Think of a situation as typical as the phone ringing. In the case of GAD, the very sound of the ringtone can cause thoughts like:

It's bad news.

The house caught fire.

Someone has died.

While this can just be characteristic of a worrywart, GAD also causes worry about things that aren't threatening or very unlikely to happen. It can also cause worry that is highly disproportional.

- Worrying about walking down a flight of stairs
- Worrying about a nuclear war
- Worrying about cancer

Here are some examples of the daily habits of someone with GAD

HABIT	WORRY
Showering with the bathroom door unlocked	In case of a fall or other emergency
Taking a longer route to school	Without highways where accidents are common
Using the bathroom frequently	To avoid peeing accidentally
Carrying a snack all the time	In case of starvation

The house catching fire? Nuclear war? Starvation? These anxieties might sound awfully exaggerated. But they are real anxieties that could occur to a GAD mind.

The GAD mind is abundant with intrusive thoughts of 'what-ifs.' Anything and everything can trigger anxiety. Much of the time, it can even feel like life itself is an anxious experience.

This causes a pattern of behaviors like:

Constant planning, just in case (carrying a lot of things for emergencies).

Avoiding uncertainty (avoiding trying something new or finding it difficult to imagine the future due to not knowing what it holds).

Trouble adjusting to change (even a small change like the seating position in a classroom can cause extreme anxiety).

Being indecisive and insecure (asking people around for reassurance about their abilities or decisions).

Being anxious all the time can be an exhausting experience. GAD takes a toll on your body and can cause physical symptoms like:

- Fatigue
- Inability to relax
- Being startled easily
- Muscle tension
- Twitching
- Trembling
- Difficulty falling asleep or staying asleep
- Nausea, diarrhea, or stomach aches

Panic disorder is characterized by frequent panic attacks or anxiety from the anticipation of a panic attack.

PANIC DISORDER

A panic attack, as mentioned earlier, is a short but intense stress response. It can be very uncomfortable, especially when we're unaware of what has triggered it. Due to the hyperventilation and rapid pulse rate during the response, it is often mistaken for a serious health problem.

The average person is likely to experience one or two panic attacks in their lifetime. A panic disorder can cause frequent panic attacks to the point that the anticipation of one causes a lot of anxiety.

Like GAD, a panic disorder can disrupt a person's routine and get in the way of living a comfortable life. It can lead to avoiding situations associated with previous panic attacks. For example, avoiding all malls because you had a panic attack at the mall once.

In extreme cases, it can lead to a condition called agoraphobia, where it becomes difficult to leave the house altogether.

Post-traumatic stress disorder (PTSD) is an anxiety disorder that follows a traumatic experience.

POST-TRAUMATIC STRESS DISORDER

PTSD is marked by episodes of anxiety triggered by reminders of the trauma. It can cause nightmares, flashbacks, dissociation (zoning out), and a feeling of panic.

A widely known example of PTSD is the experience of soldiers who have returned from war zones. Loud noises, even a car backfiring, can cause intense anxiety due to their similarity to explosives.

Similarly, PTSD can occur after a person experiences a traumatic event.

THE ANXIETY SQUAD VS. AN ANXIETY DISORDER

I'm sure many of the things we have talked about seem familiar. It can be nerve-racking to meet someone new or go to the dentist. But this does not necessarily mean that you have an anxiety disorder.

So how can you tell if it's the squad or a disorder?

Let's look at a situation that makes most of us anxious. Exams.

STUDYING FOR THE EXAM ▶

○ **Natural anxiety:** Moments of anxiety come and go.

○ **Anxiety disorder:** The upcoming exam is all you can think of to the point that you cannot study.

The anxiety is **persistent**.

◀ A DAY OR TWO BEFORE THE EXAM

○ **Natural anxiety:** You worry about your performance but feel better once you're able to recall what you've studied.

○ **Anxiety disorder:** You're convinced you're going to fail the exam and decide not to take it at all.

The anxiety is **disruptive**.

Natural anxiety: You have some anxiety.

You may have thoughts like:

Have I studied enough?

I hope I don't run out of time.

What if I forget everything I've learned?

Anxiety disorder: The anxiety is intense.

You may

- Not be able to recall anything you studied
- Feel physical symptoms of anxiety, like trembling or feeling faint

The anxiety is **overwhelming**.

Natural anxiety: The anxiety starts to come down and you're able to focus on taking the exam

Anxiety disorder: The anxiety peaks and you may

- Not be able to think clearly
- Feel panicky
- Break down
- Not be able to take the exam

The anxiety is **hard to control**.

○ **Natural anxiety:** Thoughts about your performance come and go, but you're able to get on with your day.

○ **Anxiety disorder:** You ruminate over the exam, your answers, and the possible results days after the exam is over.

The anxiety is **disproportional**.

WHEN TO WORRY ABOUT YOUR ANXIETY

You may want to examine the role of anxiety in your life if you notice changes in the following:

Mood

Sleep

Interest in doing things

Energy levels

Thoughts

Focus

Appetite

You may also notice other changes in your life:

- You are unable to feel relaxed
- You've had one or more panic attacks
- You spend a lot of time worrying
- You feel stressed out and irritable
- You often feel like something terrible is going to happen
- Your worry and stress is interfering with your life

If you suspect issues with your anxiety, you should consider sharing your concerns with someone like an adult, a parent, a school counselor, a teacher, or a trusted confidante.

CHAPTER 4

ADDRESSING

THE ANXIETY SQUAD

When the FFF response starts to malfunction, we may turn to unhealthy 'solutions.' Here are some common errors people make and how they may worsen the situation.

AVOIDANCE

You eat at a new restaurant. Something didn't quite suit you, and you're up all night with an upset stomach. Would you go back to that restaurant? Probably not.

It's the most obvious and logical thing to do. When something makes us anxious, our instincts may persuade us to avoid the source. However, this 'solution' does more harm than good in the long run.

IT STRENGTHENS THE ANXIETY.

One morning, you have a panic attack on the way to school. The next day, you avoid that route and take a different one.

The brain has made an association between that route and anxiety.

When you try to go down that route, the stress response may get triggered. The physical sensations then warn the brain of danger again, and the association grows stronger.

Every time you avoid that route, it reaffirms to the brain that going down that road is dangerous.

A BAND-AID SOLUTION AT BEST

There are many roads that lead to school. But what happens when you have another panic attack on the new route? Would the solution be to find a third route?

And if anxiety is a more common occurrence in your life, how many more things can you avoid before it starts to interfere with your routine?

RISK OF AGORAPHOBIA

Agoraphobia is defined as a fear of open spaces. However, it also refers to a condition that prevents people from leaving their homes due to anxiety.

A person with an anxiety disorder may start to avoid places and situations where they had panic attacks. They anticipate having an attack in public and gradually stop going out altogether.

Agoraphobia is when a person applies the 'avoidance' solution to everything that causes anxiety.

SAFETY BEHAVIORS

Safety behaviors are similar to avoidance tactics. They include things that people do to feel safe in situations that make them anxious.

This could be talking to someone on the phone, having someone track your movements, or carrying a totem that comforts you (like a security blanket or a teddy bear).

This behavior, like avoidance, confirms to the brain that there is a threat to be feared. And if you're unable to practice your safety behavior, your anxiety is likely to increase.

'FIXING' THE ANXIETY

A typical response to anxiety issues is to "get rid of it." But, it isn't a foreign object, and it isn't something that can be removed. It is a function that we need to survive.

It's like dealing with an upset stomach by leaving it at home before going to the restaurant. It's impossible. An antacid or a change in diet is likely to help you more.

Similarly, anxiety isn't something you rid yourself of but something you need to manage.

People may divert time and effort away from management by fixating on why they have the issue in the first place. This approach can cause negative thoughts and cause loops of anxiety.

MANAGING THE ANXIETY SQUAD

The Anxiety Squad is a part of us; we use it to function and survive. The solution to anxiety issues is not to put up a battle against them but to learn to manage them instead.

When The Anxiety Squad arrives, we go through physical sensations, thoughts, emotions, and urges to behave in a specific way. These aspects also impact each other and keep you in a loop of anxiety.

Physical sensation   Thought   Emotion   Behavior

I am terrified of heights. When I had to board my first flight, I was highly anxious.

"What if the plane crashes?"

I felt nervous and constantly asked people about their flight experiences.

I was not satisfied with the answers.
I stayed up all night ruminating.

"What if it crashes in the ocean? I don't know how to swim!"

I felt helpless. I got a weird feeling in my stomach.

I searched the internet for statistics on water landings.

I got even more afraid after reading about them.

I felt like crying.

I felt helpless, so I looked up statistics. I read about water landings and started crying.

The aspects influence and strengthen one another and keep us in a state of anxiety.

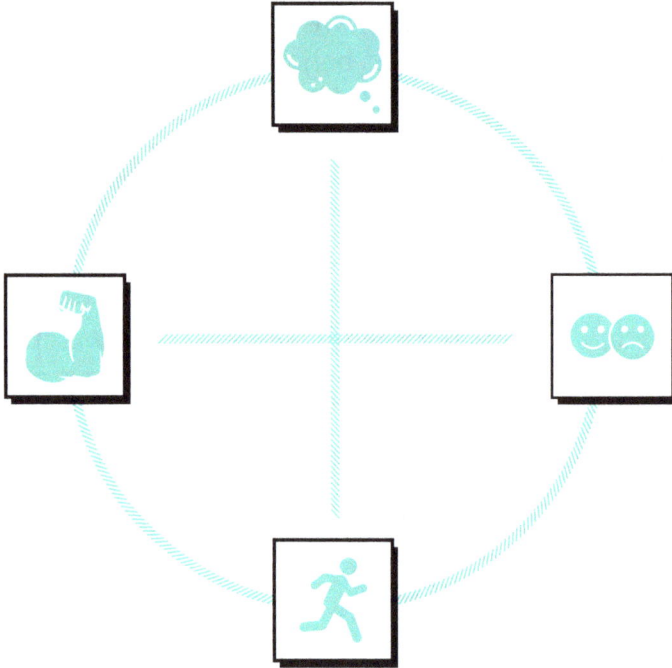

An effective way to break this momentum is to interrupt the cycle by addressing any one of these aspects - physical experience, thoughts, emotions, and behavior.

This reduces the intensity of that aspect and weakens its impact. The others follow and also begin to return to a neutral state.

There are 50 tools in this book that are divided into:

- Physical tools that use the body
- Thought tools that use the mind
- Emotion tools that build resistance
- Behavior tools that help with urges and habits

Each tool comes with the following information:

WHERE IT'S FROM

The origin of the exercise, if known

DURATION

An approximate duration

WHAT IT CAN HELP WITH

This section will include the following information:

- The level of anxiety it can help with
- Situations in which it can be beneficial
- Disorders that can be managed with the exercise

HOW TO DO IT

Step by step instructions on how to perform the exercise

WHEN TO DO IT

The ideal time or situation to do the exercise, if there is one

A VARIATION

An alternate way to perform the exercise, if there is one

Notes, if any

Looking for tools to assist someone?
Look for this symbol at the top of the page!

The tools aren't guaranteed to work for all. There might be a tool that works for your friend, but not you.

Some tools will be more effective than others. A tool may work only in certain situations, while others may require more than one tool. So, keep an open mind and experiment with them.

Try them out and see what works for you.

Think of this toolkit as a guide rather than an instruction manual. You can start by practicing the tools and eventually tailor them to your needs.

Find a tool really useful? Take a snapshot of it on your phone!

CHAPTER 5
PHYSICAL
TOOLS

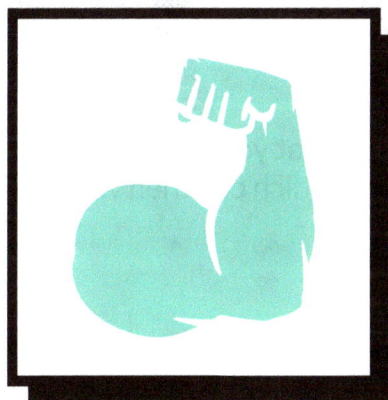

USE YOUR
BODY

The physical sensations that we experience during anxiety result from the FFF response. It isn't a switch that we consciously turn on in our brain. By the time we realize that we are feeling anxious, the response has already been triggered. There is nothing we can do to stop it from causing physical changes.

However, there are things that you can do to reduce the intensity of these physical sensations, which can then weaken the cycle and bring the anxiety to a halt.

BREATHING EXERCISES

When the fight-or-flight response is activated, our lung functions increase. This helps oxygen reach the brain faster so we can make quick decisions.

This is why when we feel anxious, overly stressed, or panicky, our breathing is affected. We may breathe very fast (hyperventilate) or not breathe deep enough (shallow breathing).

This causes an imbalance of O2 and CO2 levels in the brain, which can prolong the anxiety and even lead to a panic attack. Breathing exercises are used to break this aspect of the cycle.

CO_2 O_2

DEEP BREATHING

WHAT IT CAN HELP WITH

- Any level of anxiety

HOW TO DO IT

1

Inhale deeply through your nose.

2

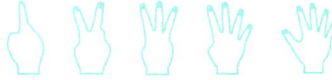

Hold it in and count one, two, three, four, five seconds.

3

Exhale slowly out of your mouth.

WHEN TO DO IT

Before, after or during anxiety

ABDOMINAL BREATHING

DURATION — As long as you need

WHAT IT CAN HELP WITH
- Any level of anxiety
- Can be used for relaxation
- Can benefit mental wellbeing when practiced regularly

HOW TO DO IT

1 Sit on a chair with your bare feet flat on the floor.

2 Find a comfortable position.

Place your hands on your belly and take deep breaths.

3 Feel the air travel into your chest and fill up your lungs.

4 Observe your belly rise and fall with every breath.

5 Concentrate on your breathing.

6 Imagine the stress leaving your body with every exhale.

A VARIATION — Instead of sitting on a chair, you can also lie down and place an open book face down on your belly. This will help you observe your belly movements.

- Before, after, or during any level of anxiety
- Regularly: as a part of your exercise routine

MINDFUL BREATHING

DURATION 3 minutes

DBT Dialectical behavior therapy

WHAT IT CAN HELP WITH

- Stress, worry and anxiety
- Can be used for relaxation
- Can benefit mental wellbeing when practiced regularly

HOW TO DO IT

1

03:00

Set a timer to three minutes.

2

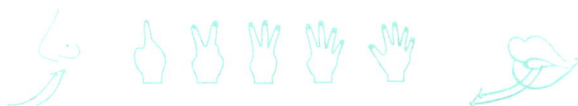

Sit in a comfortable position. Close your eyes.

Place one hand on your belly and start deep breathing.

3 **STAGE I: FOCUS**

Observe the way your stomach moves as you inhale and exhale.

Feel the air going through your nostrils and out of your mouth. If your mind wanders, it's okay. Just calmly bring your focus back to your breathing.

Immerse yourself completely in the experience by noticing all the different physical sensations.

4 STAGE II: COUNT

Start counting your breaths.

Count to four, then start again.

Try to alternate your focus between your body and the count.

4 STAGE III: FLOW

Spend some time observing your wandering mind.

Don't reason or engage with it; only observe the flow. Let the thoughts come and go

When the timer rings, open your eyes.

WHEN TO DO IT

- Before, during, or after a stressful activity
- As a part of your exercise or self-care routine

Don't be disheartened if you get distracted. The objective is not to stop your mind from wandering but to bring the focus back to your breathing.

THE FIVE-MINUTE DAILY RECHARGE PRACTICE

DURATION | 5 minutes

CBT | Cognitive-behavioral therapy

WHAT IT CAN HELP WITH
- Stress, worry and general anxiety
- Relaxation
- Mental wellbeing
- GAD

HOW TO DO IT

1 Lie down and find a comfortable position.

Start by faking some yawns until you actually yawn.

2 Close your eyes. Relax your face muscles.

Start by doing some abdominal breathing.

3 With every breath, imagine the tension leaving your body.

4 Shift your focus to the physical experience. What can you see, hear, smell, taste, and touch?

5 Feel the contact your body has with the surface on which you're on.

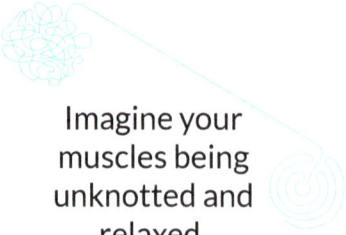

6 Imagine your muscles being unknotted and relaxed.

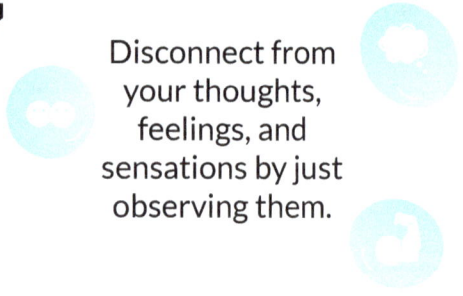

7 Disconnect from your thoughts, feelings, and sensations by just observing them.

8 Observe the rhythm of your breath.

Open your eyes when you feel relaxed.

WHEN TO DO IT
- Before, during, or after a stressful activity
- As a part of your exercise or self-care routine

GROUNDING
EXERCISES

The objective of grounding exercises is to distract yourself, focus away from the anxiety and remind yourself that you are safe and not in any danger. There are three types of grounding exercises:

- **Physical**, which involve using your senses and your body
- **Mental**, which focuses your mind
- **Self-soothing**, which is about being more empathetic towards yourself

In this section, we will explore physical grounding.

Physical grounding can help you calm down when you aren't in immediate danger, but your brain thinks you are. So... you probably don't want to use these tools if you're faced with an actual bear in the woods.

These exercises use our senses to

- Remind the brain that we are safe
- Mimic safety
- Distract ourselves

They can also be used in other situations, such as being overwhelmed with emotions like sadness or anger.

5-4-3-2-1

DURATION As long as you need

- A panic or anxiety attack
- Useful for those with GAD, social anxiety, and panic disorder

HOW TO DO IT

Count and observe:

5	4	3	2	1
things you can see	things you can feel	things you can hear	things you can smell	thing you can taste

If you don't calm down at first, 'zoom into the details' by observing more of them.

For example, if one of the five things you can see is a tree, observe:

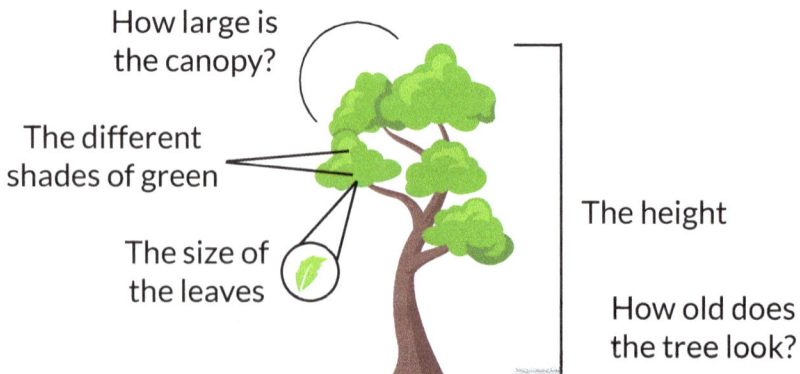

How large is the canopy?

The different shades of green

The size of the leaves

The height

How old does the tree look?

The advantage of this technique is that you can do it anywhere, whether you're alone at home, in transit, or with other people.

SAFETY RECONSTRUCTION

DBT | Dialectical behavior therapy

WHAT IT CAN HELP WITH
- A panic or anxiety attack
- Useful for those with GAD, social anxiety, and panic disorder

What is your safe space? A place that you can go to in your head where you feel safe and protected. It could be an actual place that you've been to or something from your imagination. It can include people, animals, or an activity that makes you feel secure.

HOW TO DO IT

1 Once you've decided on a safe space, find a comfortable position and close your eyes.

Imagine that you are in your safe space.

2

5	4	3	2	1

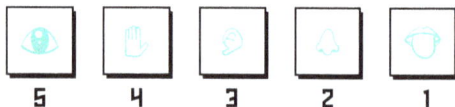

Mindfully experience what it's like to be there by doing the 5-4-3-2-1 exercise.

3

What's it like in your safe space? What can you see around you? What does the place look like?

Are there any sounds that you can hear?

Any scents that you associate with your safe space?

Are you eating something delightful there?

Are you comfortable? What's the weather like?

Continue to observe your safe space until you feel safe. You may need to zoom into the details.

When you feel safe and calm, open your eyes.

WHEN TO DO IT When you need to calm down from high levels of anxiety, or a panic attack

MIMICKING SAFETY

DURATION As long as you need

CBT Cognitive-behavioral therapy

WHAT IT CAN HELP WITH
- A panic or anxiety attack
- Useful for those with GAD, social anxiety, and panic disorder

What are the things you do when you're relaxed?

- You yawn
- You sigh
- Your body slumps into a chair
- It feels heavy and weighed down
- It feels limp and loose

HOW TO DO IT

When you're experiencing anxiety or panic, you can use your body to mimic safety and convince your brain that you are safe. Here are some ways to do that:

- Yawn and sigh forcefully
- Lift your shoulders up to your face and slowly bring them down
- Sit on a chair with a backrest. Feel your weight being pulled down by gravity.
- Find a comfortable position where you aren't consciously resting your body. Let it hang loose and limp.

WHEN TO DO IT When you need to calm down from high levels of anxiety, or a panic attack

SENSORY DISTRACTION

DURATION | As long as you need

DBT | Dialectical behavior therapy

WHAT IT CAN HELP WITH
- A panic or anxiety attack
- Useful for those with GAD, social anxiety, and panic disorder

HOW TO DO IT

There are two ways you can use your senses to distract yourself from the anxiety:

Change what your senses are experiencing. Here are some examples

Observing or counting things around you

Listening to music mindfully

Smelling coffee or vinegar

Tasting something sour or tangy

Running your hands under cold water

Distract yourself using your senses with something that you like:

Watching something pleasing to the eye like your favorite music video

Listening to your favorite song and humming/singing along

Smelling a perfume or fruit that you really like

Enjoying a morsel or meal of your favorite food

Sitting on your favorite chair or hugging a pet

If you experience anxiety or panic attacks often, it helps to have a handy list of the things you like. Make a list in a notebook or on your phone, and add to it when you think of something comforting.

WHEN TO DO IT When you need to calm down from high levels of anxiety, or a panic attack

BODY SCAN

DURATION As long as you need

CBT Cognitive-behavioral therapy

WHAT IT CAN HELP WITH
- A panic or anxiety attack
- Useful for those with GAD, social anxiety, and panic disorder

HOW TO DO IT

Observe what your body is doing and feeling. For example,

I'm sitting at a PC, writing about doing a body scan.
I feel my scalp, the hair tied into a bun.
My earphones dangling from my ears.
My glasses resting on the bridge of my nose.
The weight of my right leg on my left leg.

The smooth keyboard, the ridges on the keys S, F, and J.
My tongue resting on my teeth.

Similarly, scan your entire body, focusing on its different parts - what position are they in? How do they feel? Think of the temperature and try to notice the smallest of details.

WHEN TO DO IT When you need to calm down from high levels of anxiety, or a panic attack

SQUEEZE HUG

DURATION | As long as you need

WHAT IT CAN HELP WITH
- A panic or anxiety attack
- Useful for those with GAD, social anxiety, and panic disorder

HOW TO DO IT

1
Sit in a comfortable position.

2
Put your right palm on your left upper arm. Put your left palm on your right upper arm.

3
Squeeze yourself like you are giving yourself a hug.

Take deep breaths while doing so.

4
When you feel calm, slowly let go.

The Squeeze Hug is efficient because it helps release oxytocin or pleasure hormones in your brain.

WHEN TO DO IT | When you need to calm down from high levels of anxiety, or a panic attack

JACOBSON'S PROGRESSIVE MUSCLE RELAXATION (JPMR)

Edmund Jacobson was a physician who invented many cool things in the 1800s that we still use today.

He is the creator of biofeedback, which uses electrical sensors to monitor your body. It is still used in hospitals in electrocardiograms [ECGs] to monitor the heart and Electroencephalographies [EEGs] to observe brain waves.

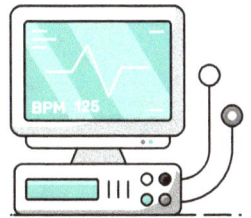

Jacobson also created a muscle relaxation exercise. It was from JPMR that the word 'relax' even came to mean 'to calm down.' JPMR can be done from the comfort of your home.

JPMR

DURATION 10-20 minutes

BY Edmund Jacobson, 1888

WHAT IT CAN HELP WITH

- Stress, worry, and general anxiety
- Relaxation
- Mental wellbeing
- GAD

HOW TO DO IT

1

Sit on a chair
(preferably with armrests).

2

Close your eyes and keep your body loose.

Start by taking 3-5 deep breaths until you begin to feel relaxed.

3

Clench one fist and hold it tightly for five seconds.

4

Then let it relax for ten seconds.

Do one hand at a time.
Keep your eyes closed and be mindful of how it feels.

Similarly, tense up the rest of your muscles (or muscle groups) one by one.

Remember, tense for five seconds, relax for ten seconds.

FACE

- Make a scowl and lower your eyebrows.
- Raise your eyebrows as high as you can.
- Close your eyes tightly.
- Tense up your jaw by putting your teeth together.
- Press your tongue against the roof of your mouth.

NECK AND SHOULDERS

- Lift your head back as far as you can.
- Bring your head down to your chest.
- Shrug your shoulders up to your ears.

TORSO

- Feel your chest filling up with air as you breathe.
- Pull your stomach in.
- Stretch and arch your back away from the chair.

ARMS

- Bend your arm at the elbow and tense your biceps.
- Straighten your arm, rest your forearms on the armrests and tense up only your triceps.

LEGS

- Squeeze your thighs (both of them simultaneously) and buttocks together.
- Point your toes towards your head to tense up your calves.
- Point your toes away from your head.
- Curl your toes down.

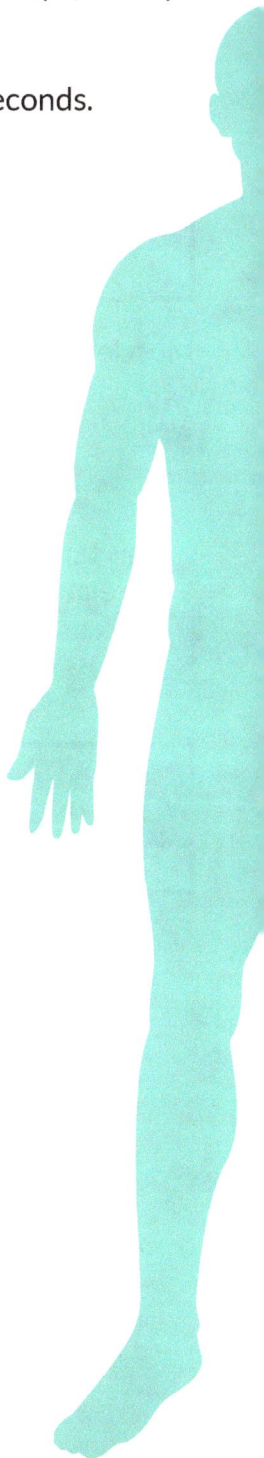

6  Relax the entire body by sinking down into your chair.	7 Stay in that moment for a minute or so. Open your eyes slowly. Stretch before you stand up.

Muscle tension is a common symptom of anxiety. JPMR can help you deal with this symptom, relaxing your body and therefore your mind as well.

This technique is beneficial for those who feel like they're unable to relax physically at all. Regular practice can train the body to relax as a response to muscle tension.

WHEN TO DO IT

- Before, after, or during any level of anxiety
- Regularly: as a part of your exercise routine or before bedtime

DIET, SLEEP, AND EXERCISE

While nothing we can eat to instantly turn off the fight-or-flight mode, diet and exercise can reduce potential anxiety.

DIET

What we eat affects how our body and brain function. Remember how we talked about cortisol and adrenaline being released during the stress response?

Some foods, like those containing sugar and caffeine, can also cause the release of these hormones.

So it helps to have these foods in moderation. Try reducing your intake to see how much sugar or caffeine you can have without the stress response going off.

Whole grains and sweet root vegetables can help balance your nervous system. Sweet root vegetables include carrots, sweet potatoes, butternut squash, onions, and parsnips.

Harmful substances like nicotine, alcohol, and other intoxicants can also contribute to anxiety. They affect your heart rate, blood pressure and activate certain neurotransmitters in your brain. Turning to these substances to cope with anxiety can also put you at risk of addiction.

SLEEP

Zzz

Sleeping is like running updates on our operating software, i.e., our brain and body.

60% complete

While we're asleep, our brain consolidates all the information that we've collected that day. This helps with memory, focus, and problem-solving.

Our body also requires sleep to repair itself. This is why you feel exhausted when you're unwell since all those white blood cells are hard at work.

A healthy sleep schedule includes:

Going to bed and waking up at roughly the same time every day

08:00:00

Aiming for a minimum of eight hours of sleep

Be aware that, as a teenager, you may have trouble sticking to a sleep schedule. This is because the hormonal changes during puberty also affect your sleep.

So, cut yourself some slack if you cannot keep up with these guidelines.

However, here are some things that can help you fall asleep faster:

ONE HOUR BEFORE BEDTIME

Avoid using electronic devices with backlights because they fool your brain into thinking it's still daytime and you don't need to go to bed.

Avoid stimulating your brain with activities like studying, playing video games, or anything that requires a lot of focus.

Our brains shut down gradually, so keeping the brain active until bedtime can make it harder to fall asleep.

STILL UNABLE TO FALL ASLEEP?

Increase the amount of physical activity during the day. You may need to exhaust your body a little more so it will want to sleep.

Use a bedtime story. Bedtime stories help you find a resting place for that wandering mind. There are plenty of bedtime story audios available online.

Use a sleep meditation guide. A meditation guide is an audio track in which a soothing voice guides you to relax your body so you can fall asleep.

EXERCISE

Exercise can be a double-pronged approach to tackling anxiety:

- It releases endorphins, which are feel-good chemicals that can significantly improve general mental wellbeing

- It can use the extra adrenaline and cortisol released during the stress response.

If traditional exercise is not your style, you can try:

Yoga

Dancing

Hula hoop

Sports

 Outdoor activities like hiking, trekking, rock climbing, and swimming

You can also incorporate physical activity into your routine by doing the following:

 Take the stairs instead of an elevator

 Walk while you talk on the phone

 Walk or cycle to school instead of driving or taking the bus

 Use a standing desk

CHAPTER 6 THOUGHT TOOLS

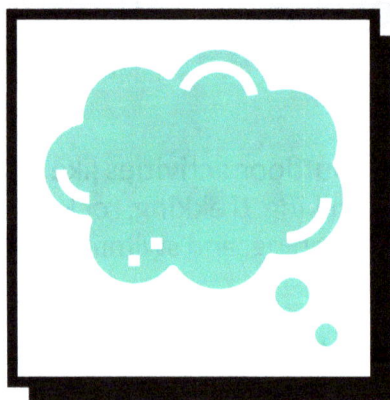

USE YOUR MIND

Our thoughts are like trains that travel faster than our lips can move. They're always around and can affect physical sensations, emotions, and behavior:

- You can get the heebie-jeebies at the thought of creepy crawlies.

- You can feel sad just by thinking of someone.

- You may think you have no chance of winning a contest, so decide not to even participate.

Thoughts may seem to come out of nowhere, like an internal monolog that's providing meaningless commentary. However, thinking is an active process that is part of cognition.

Cognition is a term used to describe our brains' activities, like thinking, knowing, remembering, and problem-solving. It helps us do pretty much everything - from tying shoelaces to solving algebraic equations.

THOUGHTS AND ANXIETY

Thoughts play a significant role when it comes to anxiety. They offer fuel for the anxiety by pointing out all the things that could go wrong. They remind us of everything we need to worry about. They can even suggest we worry about things we don't need to worry about. They relay information that can keep us in a state of anxiety.

And because they're constantly with us, they can play a huge role in triggering and prolonging anxiety.

There are four ways we can address anxiety by using our minds:

- **Thought challenging** - Reasoning with irrational thoughts
- **Acceptance techniques** - Using thoughts to accept and cope
- **Defusion techniques** - Distancing ourselves from our thoughts
- **Thought grounding** - Reminding ourselves that we are safe using our thoughts

THOUGHT CHALLENGING

Thinking is like any other cognitive process. Sometimes, we lapse in memory and forget to return a phone call.

Similarly, we are bound to make mistakes while thinking and can have irrational thoughts.

Here are ten types of irrational thinking. Can you figure out what their descriptions are?

Note: Only one answer per type

	TYPE OF THINKING		DESCRIPTION
1	Catastrophizing	A	Branding a person or situation
2	All or nothing	B	Setting rigid expectations for yourself or others
3	Discounting	C	If you feel something, it must be true
4	Labeling	D	Making assumptions about how others regard you
5	Personalizing	E	Accepting responsibility for something you did not cause or making a situation about yourself

6	Should, must, and ought to	F	Thinking in extremes
7	Fortune telling	G	Painting people or events with the same brush
8	Mind reading	H	Jumping to the worst-case scenario
9	Emotional reasoning	I	Predicting how things are going to turn out
10	Overgeneralizing	J	Looking at the negatives and not counting the positives

Did any of them sound familiar? Have you arrived at an irrational thought at some point?

Here's a list of the processes with examples and identifiers:

TYPE OF THINKING	IDENTIFIER	EXAMPLE
Catastrophizing	I'm going to… (worst-case scenario)	I'm going to fail and be homeless in the future I'm going to have a heart attack and die
	What if	What if the plane crashes? What if the dog bites me and I get rabies?
All or nothing	Always, never, all, no(o)ne, everything, nothing	I always mess up No one loves me Everything is going wrong
Discounting	Making excuses to disregard the positive But that doesn't count It's not the same thing	I know I did better last time, but that doesn't count That was a completely different situation; it's not the same thing
Labeling	I'm such a _____	I'm such an idiot
	They're such a _____	They're such morons
Personalizing	Blaming yourself	It's all my fault
	Putting yourself in tragic situations (what if)	I'm the same age, what if it happens to me? I live in the same area; what if I get robbed?

		I should not fail
Should, must, and ought to	Using definitive language to describe shortcomings	They must listen to me
		I ought to be less careless
Fortune telling	It happened once, it will happen again	I'm going to fail again
	It's in my stars	It's me; something has to go wrong
Mind reading	They think _____	They think I'm weird
	They ____ me	They don't like me
Emotional reasoning	I feel _____ so I must be _____	I feel ugly, so I'm ugly
	But I feel...	But I feel bad
Overgeneralizing	One instance is evidence for all	I failed once, so I will always fail
	They are all the same	I don't trust <group> because one of them lied to me

Irrational thoughts like these are a common byproduct of emotion, and it's natural for them to come and go.

You may stub your toe and think "Ugh, I'm so clumsy." It happens to all of us.

However, irrational thoughts can play a somewhat villainous role in anxiety.

Remember the thoughts that can occur with social anxiety?

Let's explore this one:

They think I'm a loser.

Can you figure out the type of thinking that resulted in the thoughts?

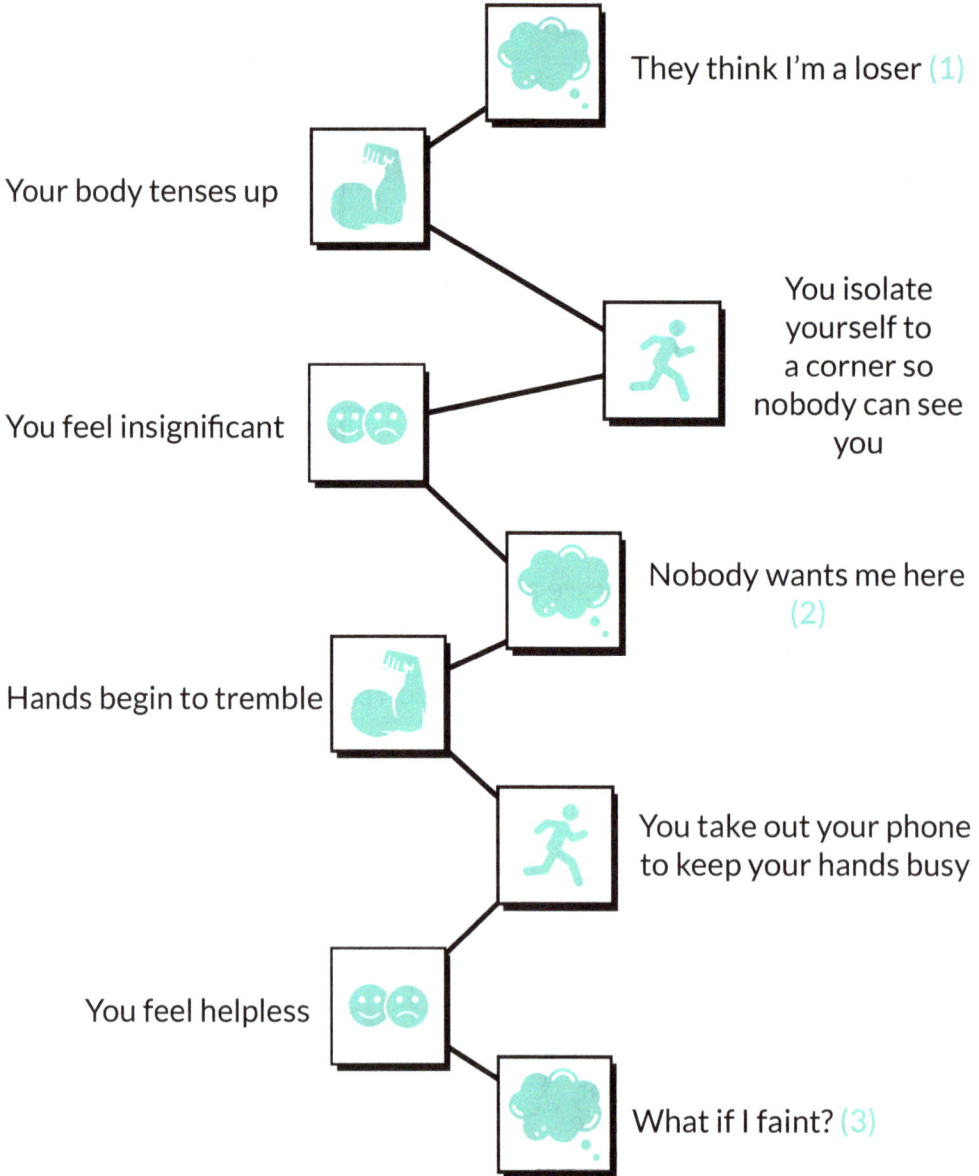

They think I'm a loser (1)

Your body tenses up

You isolate yourself to a corner so nobody can see you

You feel insignificant

Nobody wants me here (2)

Hands begin to tremble

You take out your phone to keep your hands busy

You feel helpless

What if I faint? (3)

Thoughts play this role in any amount of anxiety. You don't need to have an anxiety disorder to experience them.

A relatable example is constantly thinking about something that worries or stresses you out, despite knowing how bad it makes you feel. Every time the thought occurs, it strengthens the anxiety.

Another way that thoughts can impact anxiety is that they tend to multiply. One irrational thought can lead to another irrational thought and take us down a spiral of unhealthy thinking.

One of the most valuable methods to curb anxiety is challenging these irrational thoughts and replacing them with coping thoughts.

THOUGHT RECORD

DURATION | 5 minutes

CBT | Cognitive-behavioral therapy

WHAT IT CAN HELP WITH

Get into the habit of:

- **R**ecognizing irrational thoughts
- **E**xamining why they're irrational
- **C**hanging the narrative

HOW TO DO IT

Use a notebook or your phone for this tool. Make seven columns with the following headings:

- The trigger
- Reaction [emotion and behavior]
- Irrational thoughts
- Justification [Evidence that the thought is true]
- Contradiction [Evidence that the thought is false]
- Balanced thought
- Learning

Here's a description of what you should write under each heading:

THE TRIGGER

Choose a trigger where you had irrational thoughts and then describe it.

This could be a situation, a memory, a photograph, a song, a person.

REACTION [EMOTION AND BEHAVIOR]

How did you feel? How intense was it? What did you do?

Write down your emotions in any form. You can use a rating, percentages, descriptions, or just list them out.

Also, write down how you reacted. Did you cry? Yell at someone? Did you isolate yourself?

IRRATIONAL THOUGHTS

List the different thoughts that are/were running through your mind.

Rate them according to their intensity.

Which thought was persistent?

Circle it. This is the thought that you will keep in mind as you fill out the rest of the column.

JUSTIFICATION [Evidence that the thought *is true*]

What justifies this thought?

For example, you're going to travel by airplane and constantly think, "What if the plane crashes?"

Yes, there is a slight chance that the plane could crash.

Planes have crashed before.

CONTRADICTION [Evidence that the thought *is false*]

What evidence is there that opposes the thought?

Plane crashes are rare.

Flying is the safest mode of mass transportation.

Aircraft are thoroughly tested before they are put to use.

The airline company will ensure that the flight is safe, as they may be sued if something goes wrong.

BALANCED THOUGHT

Rephrase the thought by considering both the evidence for and against it.

"I am afraid of flying. However, the chance of a plane crash is meager. I can trust the airline and will have a safe flight even though I am anxious."

LEARNING

Read the columns from the beginning and see if you learned anything from the exercise.

How would you rephrase the irrational thoughts?

How would you have reacted had you done this exercise at the time?

Is there any way to apply this tactic to other persistent, irrational thoughts you may have in the future?

You can erase or delete it when you're finished if you want.

Think of this exercise like training wheels on a bicycle. You do it on paper until you get into the habit of doing it mentally.

Once you get the hang of it, you can use it to challenge an irrational thought at any time.

The basic idea of thought challenging is to find evidence to justify and contradict the irrational thought to get clarity on the situation. You can then change the perspective, rephrase the thought and avoid spiraling into anxiety.

Here are some exercises that you can use to challenge irrational thoughts. To help you out, we've included the type of thinking that these exercises can help with.

PUTTING YOUR THOUGHTS ON TRIAL

DURATION 5 minutes

CBT Cognitive-behavioral therapy

WHAT IT CAN HELP WITH

- Any irrational thinking style

HOW TO DO IT

Imagine you are in a courtroom when you have an irrational thought, and your thoughts are on trial.

This exercise is evidence-based, like maintaining the Thought RECord. However, it includes an observer's opinion. You take a moment to examine the situation and the resulting thought from an outsider's perspective.

Let's use this thought:

Nobody likes me.

How would the prosecutor prove that nobody likes you?

How would the lawyer defend you and prove that someone actually likes you?

JUSTIFICATION

CONTRADICTION

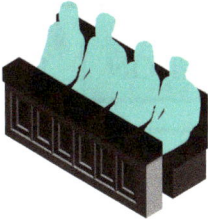

What does the jury think
of the evidence they're
presented with?

THIRD-PARTY PERSPECTIVE

What is the verdict?

BALANCED THOUGHT

CONTINUUM V1.0

DURATION 10 minutes

CBT Cognitive-behavioral therapy

WHAT IT CAN HELP WITH

- Labeling

HOW TO DO IT

Imagine or draw a straight line with percentages on either side. Rate yourself or the person the thought refers to. For example,

I am a horrible person.

0% ———————————————————————— 100%

50%

Now make a list of criteria for the 0% and the 100% sides.

0% HORRIBLE	100% HORRIBLE
- Empathetic - Cares about others - Kind - Helpful	- Doesn't care about anyone else - Hurts other people on purpose - Is rude and mean - Is selfish

Remember, these are just examples. You decide the criteria for 0% and 100%.

Now reflect back on the thought and re-evaluate yourself on the scale.

DURATION 10 minutes

CBT Cognitive-behavioral therapy

WHAT IT CAN HELP WITH

- Labeling

HOW TO DO IT

This version of the continuum uses antonyms instead of a scale. You rate yourself or another person using the scale, but instead of listing criteria, you use a contrasting list of words. For example,

0%   100%

Completely awful	Totally awesome
Offensive	Respectful
Selfish	Helpful
Lazy	Productive
Spiteful	Considerate
Biased	Fair
Cruel	Compassionate
Abusive	Empathetic
Indifferent	Caring
Dishonest	Honest
Hostile	Hospitable

(Add your own words according to whatever you value)

Start with an initial belief and then re-evaluate after you rate yourself using this continuum.

BACK TO THE PRESENT

CBT | Cognitive-behavioral therapy

WHAT IT CAN HELP WITH
- Fortune telling
- What-ifs

HOW TO DO IT

Take a piece of paper and draw this:

Past _____ Future

Present

Place your finger on the point of time that your thought focuses on. For example,

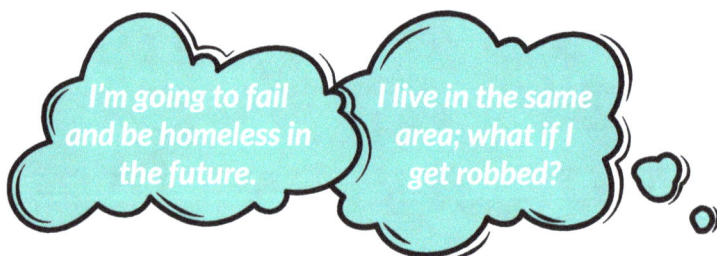

> I'm going to fail and be homeless in the future.

> I live in the same area; what if I get robbed?

Since these are thoughts about the future, you would place your finger on 'future.'

> I failed once, so I will always fail.

> "It's me; something has to go wrong."

Bring your focus back to the present. Slide your finger up or down the line and then to the present, depending on the thought. When you arrive at the present, rephrase the thought. For example,

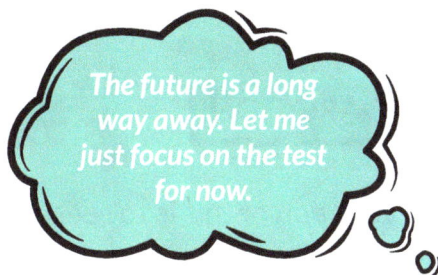

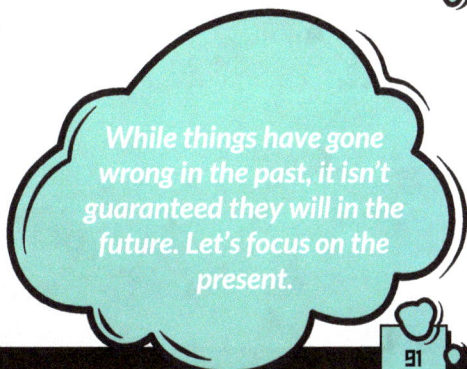

I'm going to fail and be homeless in the future.

→

The future is a long way away. Let me just focus on the test for now.

I live in the same area; what if I get robbed?

→

I can't predict what is going to happen. All I can do is be a little more careful.

I failed once, so I will always fail

→

Just because it happened once, it does not mean it will always happen. Things can and do change.

It's me; something has to go wrong.

→

While things have gone wrong in the past, it isn't guaranteed they will in the future. Let's focus on the present.

Anxious thoughts have the tendency to jump across time, cooking up worst-case scenarios or bringing up old painful memories. Visualizing and interacting with the restlessness of your thoughts can help bring your focus back to the present.

A VARIATION

A variation of this is to see where the source of your anxiety lies. For example,

What if the dog bites me and I get rabies?

In the present, you have not been bitten by a dog, and you don't have rabies. So who should address this problem? Past you? Present you? Or future you?

Past   Present   Future ✓

Similarly, when anxiety pulls up a socially awkward moment from your past, ask yourself who had to deal with the embarrassment? Past you? Present you? Or future you?

Past   Present   Future

SO WHAT IF?

CBT/DBT Cognitive-behavioral therapy/ Dialectical behavior therapy

WHAT IT CAN HELP WITH
- What-ifs

HOW TO DO IT

A lot of anxiety is generated from sentences that start with 'What if...'

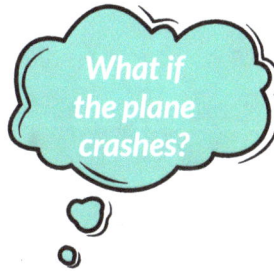

What if the dog bites me?

What if the plane crashes?

What if someone makes fun of me?

This exercise is composed of two parts. Let's use the first example.

1 Assess the likelihood of the possibility of the event occurring.

- What if the dog bites me - 40%
- What if I get rabies - 5%
- What if the wound gets infected and they've got to amputate my leg - .0001%

We then eliminate those situations that aren't likely to happen, such as the worst-case scenarios: rabies and amputation.

2 Now we explore the most likely scenario:

- So what if the dog bites me?
- I can call for medical help.
- There are injections I can be given to prevent rabies.
- The dog has probably already been vaccinated.
- You can't die from a dog bite. I'll be okay.

PIE CHARTS

CBT Cognitive-behavioral therapy

WHAT IT CAN HELP WITH ▪ Irrational thoughts of guilt, embarrassment, and blame

HOW TO DO IT

This exercise uses pieces of a pie chart to dissect the irrational thought and accept that the subject of the thought results from a lot more than just you.

You start with the initial belief.

For example, after a piano recital gone wrong, you think:

> *I always mess up.*

1 List all the factors that led to the mistake and assign a percentage to each.

- "I was nervous."
- "It was my first solo recital."
- "I am not used to the spotlight."
- "I've only been learning piano for a year."

2 Use these factors to make a pie chart. You can imagine one or even use an app or website to create one.

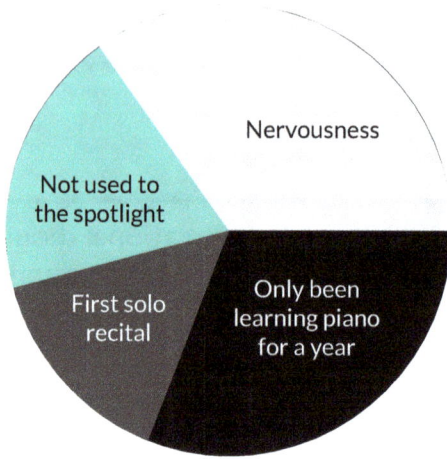

The pie chart in the example suggests that you don't 'always' mess up. It also illustrates that other things played a role, and all of it didn't depend on how you play the piano.

ACCEPTANCE TECHNIQUES

Thoughts have the tendency to circle back to a problem every now and then. It was probably helpful for our ancestors to be reminded to shift camp to a warmer place as winter approached. But recurring thoughts today tend to be about an embarrassing incident from your past or something you need to worry about ten years from now.

Acceptance techniques are ways to accept a situation or circumstance, so the thought reduces frequency or intensity.

CIRCLE OF CONTROL

DURATION 5-10 minutes

The 7 Habits of Highly Effective People, by Stephen Covey

WHAT IT CAN HELP WITH

- Anxiety, worry and stress

HOW TO DO IT

Think of a recurring worry or something that is a constant source of stress. This could be an upcoming exam, the health of a relative, or a plan for the future.

For example, your school band has a performance coming up.

1 On a piece of paper, draw a circle in the middle. This is your circle of control. In this circle, list all the things in your control.

CIRCLE OF CONTROL

How you play your instrument

How much you can practice

How many hours a day you can dedicate to it

Asking others how you can improve

2 Now we draw a circle around the circle of control. This is your circle of influence. How can you influence the situation?

CIRCLE OF INFLUENCE

Ask the rest of the band to practice

Suggest more rehearsals

Ask your teacher to instruct them to practice more

3 Now we draw a third circle around the circle of influence. This is your circle of concern. Here is where you would put away thoughts about things that you can neither control nor influence.

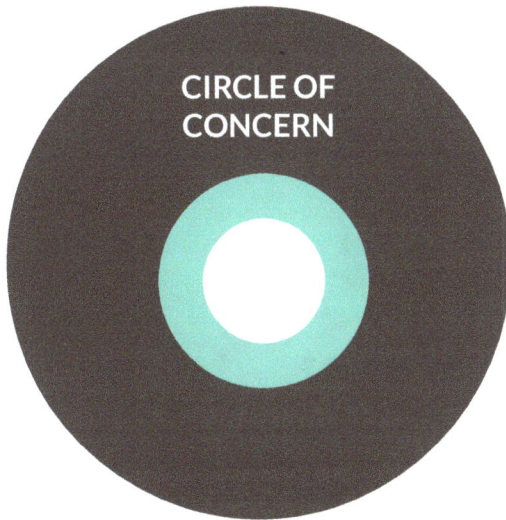

CIRCLE OF CONCERN

What if a string breaks?

What if there's a storm and nobody can attend?

What if there's a power outage?

The Circle of Control is used to understand the limitations of our control and influence so we can remind ourselves that we've done enough.

Another way to do this exercise is to imagine three boxes - control, influence, and concern.

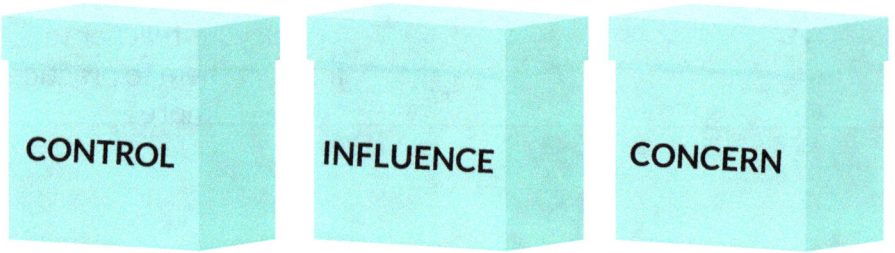

CONTROL   **INFLUENCE**   **CONCERN**

Imagine sorting things into these boxes every time you have an anxious thought.

DURATION 1-3 minutes

CBT Cognitive-behavioral therapy

WHAT IT CAN HELP WITH
- Stress management

HOW TO DO IT

A worry tree is similar to the circle of control. You visualize a flowchart of your worries and what you can do about them.

Start with the base of a tree. What are you worried about? Be specific. For example,

I am worried about my driving test.

Then, ask yourself if there is anything you can do about it and add branches to the tree.

NO
Change focus

YES
Practice driving

If there is nothing you can do about it, change focus by doing a grounding exercise. If there is something you can do, go ahead and do it. But if a new worry crops up, continue the exercise.

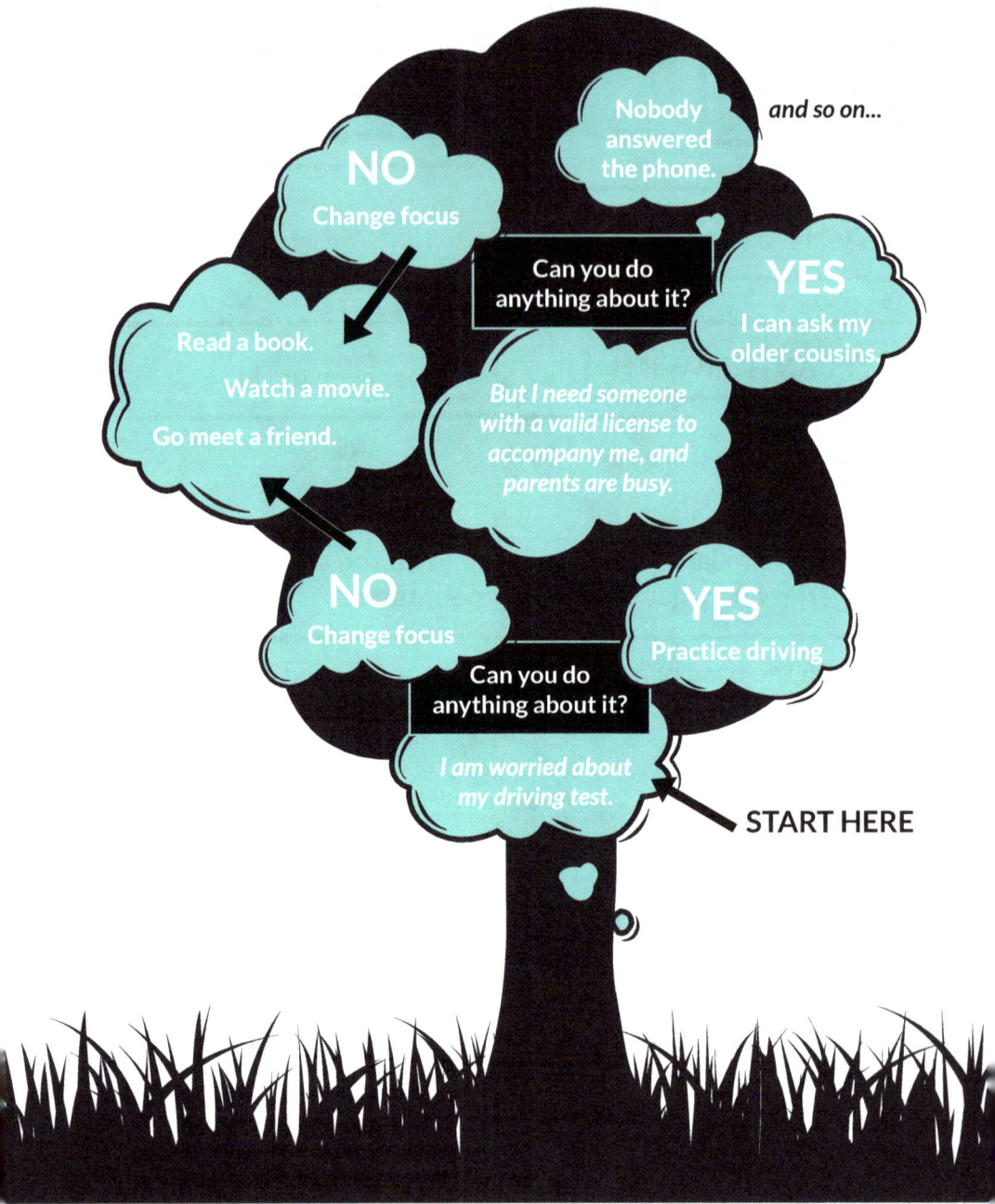

This can help you tick off the things you are worrying about and know that you have indeed addressed everything.

| WHEN TO DO IT | When you have a recurring worrying thought |

SEMANTIC SATIATION

ACT Acceptance-Commitment Therapy

WHAT IT CAN HELP WITH
- Irrational thoughts

HOW TO DO IT

Semantic - related to words and language
Satiation - satisfying yourself until you are full

Chances are, you have done this before. When we repeat a word too many times, it stops making sense. This phenomenon is known as semantic satiation.

This can be used to take power away from an irrational thought. For example,

I am ugly. Iam ugly. Iamugly. Iamugly. Iamugly.

Say it over and over until it stops making sense. I personally did it, and I am now Mugly.

I am Mugly.

SOUND MANIPULATION

ACT Acceptance-Commitment Therapy

WHAT IT CAN HELP WITH

- Irrational thoughts

HOW TO DO IT

Similar to semantic satiation, this tool changes the sound of the thought to take away its meaning.

You can do this by speeding up or slowing down the way you say the thought.

You can even record the thought and then play it back to yourself at different speeds or even backward.

TRANSLATE IT!

DURATION 3-5 minutes

ACT Acceptance-Commitment Therapy

WHAT IT CAN HELP WITH
- Irrational thoughts

HOW TO DO IT

Another tool that helps disconnect the thought from its meaning is hearing it or saying it in a language you don't know.

You can use a translator and pick a language that sounds very different from those you are familiar with.

For example, I translated 'I am ugly' into Sinhalese and this doesn't sound as unsettling as the original thought.

Mama ketayi.

COGNITIVE REAPPRAISAL

DURATION | 1-3 minutes

CBT | Cognitive-behavioral therapy

WHAT IT CAN HELP WITH

- Any level of anxiety

HOW TO DO IT

This tool uses a change of perspective by rephrasing the thought. For example,

Oh no, I'm very anxious.

This thought suggests that something is wrong and can keep you in a state of anxiety. To use this tool, you consciously rephrase the thought to a less negative one:

My anxiety is just a little high right now. It'll be fine soon.

This reminds you that what you're going through is natural and nothing to worry about.

You can also label the response to normalize the experience.

Here are some examples of how to do this:

Oh, my brain is just picking up the wrong signal again!

Oops, I've activated my FFF response.

RADICAL ACCEPTANCE

Radical acceptance is finding a balance between accepting a situation and recognizing how you can produce a different outcome in the future. It is radical because you don't fight it or hurry out of it; you stand in the face of it and say, "Okay."

It's like getting caught in the rain. The first few moments, you may run around looking for shelter, but the wetter you get, the more you accept it.

Okay, I guess I'm getting drenched today!

With anxiety, you understand all of the factors that have led to the situation. You acknowledge that while it makes you feel anxious, you can do nothing to change what has already happened.

RADICALLY ACCEPT A SITUATION

DURATION 5-10 minutes

DBT Dialectical behavior therapy

WHAT IT CAN HELP WITH

- Anxiety about the past

HOW TO DO IT

1 The first part of radically accepting a situation or circumstance is recognizing the chain of events that led up to a situation.

Think back to the cause of the situation and then think back to the cause of that, and so on. For example,

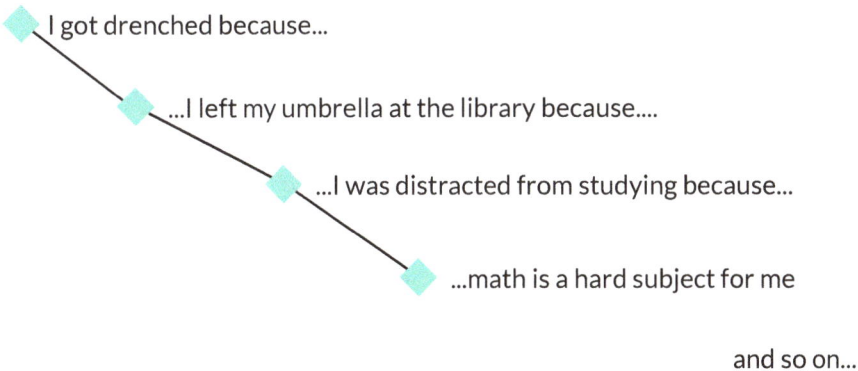

I got drenched because...

...I left my umbrella at the library because....

...I was distracted from studying because...

...math is a hard subject for me

and so on...

Or you can chronologically chart the events out like a timeline or even a chain linked together.

2 Once you have a perspective of the situation from a much wider lens, replace the anxious thought with a coping thought:

This, too, shall pass.

This is only temporary.

The circumstances aren't pleasant.

These feelings won't kill me.

It is natural for me to feel this way.

I'm just feeling anxious right now.

It is what it is.

RADICALLY ACCEPT YOURSELF

DURATION 5-10 minutes

DBT Dialectical behavior therapy

WHAT IT CAN HELP WITH

- Irrational thoughts about yourself
- Social anxiety
- Improving self-esteem and confidence

HOW TO DO IT

1 A lot of irrational thoughts are assumptions about ourselves. In moments of high emotion, we tend to judge ourselves with a very harsh lens.

Replacing thoughts like "I'm such a loser" or "I always mess up" with coping thoughts can reduce the chance of a downward spiral through all the mistakes you've ever made. Here are some coping thoughts that you can use:

I made a mistake

I'm not perfect

I'm doing the best I can

I'm not defined by my mistakes

I am good at some things, and I'm working on the others

My experience of the world is my own

I take responsibility for my actions

THOUGHT DEFUSION

Just like you defuse a bomb to prevent it from exploding, defusion techniques are used to reduce the impact of negative thoughts and emotions.

THOUGHT DEFUSION

DURATION 3-5 minutes

ACT Acceptance-commitment therapy   **CBT** Cognitive behavioral therapy

WHAT IT CAN HELP WITH

- Irrational thoughts
- Recurring and intrusive thoughts

HOW TO DO IT

1 Lie down or just sit comfortably with your eyes closed.

Imagine a scenario where things pass by one after the other.

These things could be
billboards passing by as you drive on a highway,
leaves flowing down a calm stream,
the end credits of a movie, or something familiar to you.

2 Imagine that your thoughts are written on what you chose and are passing by you.

Do not stop at a thought or judge yourself for having that thought; just let them go.

If you find yourself getting hooked on a thought, simply remember to disengage and send it on its way.

If two thoughts appear at once, let them come and go together.

3 After 3-5 minutes, take a few deep breaths, open your eyes and bring your focus back to where you are.

MEDITATION

DURATION As long as you need

YOGA Earliest reference: 1000-500 BCE

WHAT IT CAN HELP WITH

■ Anxiety, stress, worry, distress

HOW TO DO IT

Meditation is a technique where you use mindfulness and focus to distract yourself from the distress and achieve calmness.

You can meditate by yourself while sitting comfortably or lying down. You can use an app or guided audiovisual aids.

Sometimes, anxiety itself can stand in the way of meditation. The racing thoughts can take center stage and fuel the anxiety. In these situations, it helps to channel the focus on:

AN OBJECT

like the flame of the candle

AN ACTIVITY

Doodling

Coloring

Exercise

Playing an instrument

Cleaning

MENTAL GROUNDING

Remember the physical grounding exercises? You used your senses to engage with the world around you and distract yourself from the anxiety. Similarly, mental grounding uses your thoughts to divert focus away from the anxiety.

REMEMBER, REMEMBER

DURATION 3-5 minutes

DBT Dialectical behavior therapy

WHAT IT CAN HELP WITH
- Any type of anxiety

HOW TO DO IT

Choose a pleasant and vivid memory. It could be a holiday, a party or just any good time!

Close your eyes and try to remember all the details.

Where were you? What did you do?

Who were you with? Do you remember what they were wearing?

What did your environment look like? What was the weather like?

Remember as much as you can and paint the picture in your mind. When you are feeling calmer, open your eyes.

DAYDREAM

DURATION 3-5 minutes

DBT Dialectical behavior therapy

WHAT IT CAN HELP WITH

- Any type of anxiety

HOW TO DO IT

Close your eyes and let your imagination run wild. Bring to life one of your fantasies by focusing on it. For example:

You won an Oscar!

What is your acceptance speech? What are you wearing? Who are you going to thank?

You are a superhero and need to fight an enemy.

What are your superpowers? Who is the villain? How will you outsmart them?

You're in a music video of a song you really like - what's it like? Do you have backup dancers?

(In my imaginary music videos, I'm always driving!)

When you are feeling calmer, open your eyes and return to reality.

COUNTING

DURATION 3-5 minutes

DBT Dialectical behavior therapy

WHAT IT CAN HELP WITH

■ Any type of anxiety

HOW TO DO IT

This tool is used to occupy your mind with math. Think of a rule and start counting accordingly. Here are some examples:

■ Count backward from 100 by subtracting 7 each time

100-93-86-79....

■ Count only in multiples of three

3-6-9-12-15-18-21...

You can make up any rule. Try to pick something that is between easy and difficult. It should challenge you enough to distract you but not so much that it overwhelms or frustrates you.

A VARIATION

If you're on the road, you can add up the numbers of the license plates of vehicles passing by.

CATEGORIES

WHAT IT CAN HELP WITH

- Any type of anxiety

HOW TO DO IT

Think of a category and fill it with as many things you can think of. Here are some examples:

- Fictional characters starting with the letter L (or any letter)

  Loki
  Luke Skywalker
  Legolas and so on

- Fantasy movies

  Fantastic beasts and where to find them
  How to train your dragon
  Brave and so on

A VARIATION

Want to make it more interesting? List items in alphabetical order. For example, breeds of dogs from A-Z:

Alaskan husky
Beagle
Collie
Dalmation and so on

CHAPTER 7
EMOTION
TOOLS

BUILD YOUR
RESISTANCE

Emotions. They are unavoidable, and you can try to force yourself not to feel, but it's not likely to work. And even when you think you don't have emotions, you are apathetic, which is also an emotion.

And when it comes to anxiety, the challenge is that anxiety itself is an emotion. The goal of these exercises is not about changing the emotion but about building resistance to it by understanding it better.

UNDERSTANDING YOUR ANXIETY

As we mentioned earlier, anxiety is a unique experience, and no two people will experience it the exact same way. So it is helpful to understand your own brand of anxiety.

EMOTION RECOGNITION

DURATION 3-5 minutes

DBT Dialectical behavior therapy

WHAT IT CAN HELP WITH
- Recognizing accompanying emotions

HOW TO DO IT

When you're anxious, you may experience other emotions that crop up in response, like helplessness, guilt, shame, or even anger, and feel overwhelmed by the experience.

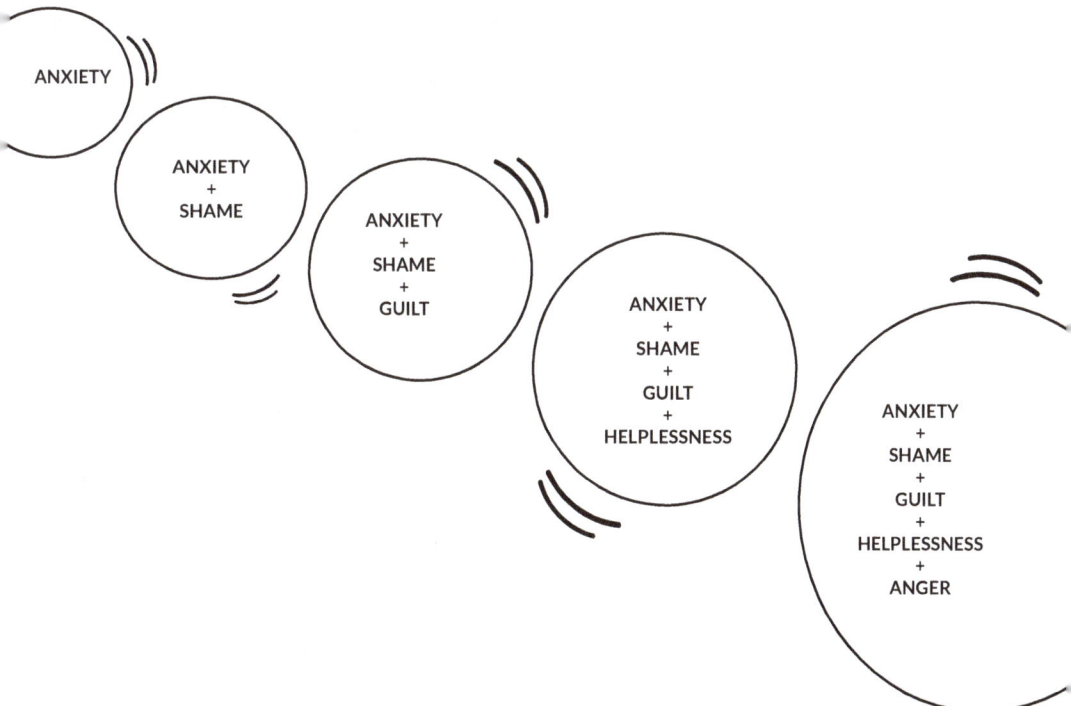

ANXIETY

ANXIETY
+
SHAME

ANXIETY
+
SHAME
+
GUILT

ANXIETY
+
SHAME
+
GUILT
+
HELPLESSNESS

ANXIETY
+
SHAME
+
GUILT
+
HELPLESSNESS
+
ANGER

While you can't stop the anxiety, you can prevent the accompanying emotions from causing a pile-up.

For example, when you feel shame due to anxiety, you aim to understand its origin and not let it snowball into the other emotions. Do this by answering 6 questions about your anxious experience:

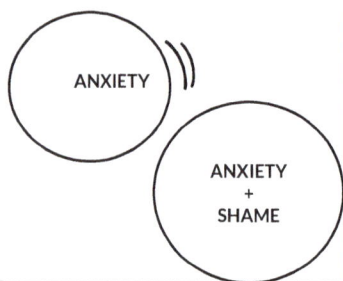

- What happened?
- Why did it happen?
- What was the primary emotion, and what were the emotions in response to it?
- What did you feel like doing?
- What did you end up doing?
- What were the consequences?

ANXIETY

ANXIETY + SHAME

This exercise will give you clarity on the experience and enable you to cope better in the future.

The next time you feel shame during anxiety, you can attribute it to anxiety and prevent it from escalating.

WHEN TO DO IT After experiencing anxiety

WHAT IT CAN HELP WITH

■ Clear up the chaos of anxiety

HOW TO DO IT

This tool is about using journaling to better understand your anxieties. When you put down your worries and feelings on paper, it can offer some clarity and disrupt anxiety's chaos.

You can journal in a way that is comfortable for you. There are no rules.

It could be a notebook, a document on your pc/ phone, or an online journal. You can save what you've written or delete it when you're done; it's up to you.

You can also decide how you want to document what you're experiencing.

● It can be
● bullet points
● with keywords,

drawings, song lyrics, or poetry.

You can even organize them into ⟍boxes⟍ ⟨or⟩charts⟩

WHAT SHOULD YOU JOURNAL ABOUT?

It can be helpful to note down the thoughts you're having, the other emotions you're experiencing, what you feel like doing and what could happen if you do.

Remember, these are just cues; you should journal whatever you feel like journaling.

WHEN TO DO IT   During or after an anxious experience

MOOD TRACKING

WHAT IT CAN HELP WITH

■ Identifying triggers

HOW TO DO IT

Mood tracking is charting out the change in your moods throughout the day. You can do this using a journal* or with an app.

You wake up and write down the emotions that you're feeling.

7 am   Bored, neutral, meh

If you feel a change in your mood throughout the day, document it, along with the time and activity.

10 am   Surprise test   Nervous, helpless

This can help you determine if there is a pattern to your anxieties:

■ Are there emotions that precede anxiety?
■ What are the usual suspects that accompany anxiety?
■ Is there a time of day or activity during which you're more anxious?

*Check out our journals at www.teen-thrive.com

BUILDING RESISTANCE

When you have an anxiety disorder, anxiety can become commonplace. While you may be getting help to deal with the triggers, it can be helpful to strengthen your tolerance so that the anxiety isn't disruptive.

EMOTION DEFUSION

DURATION 5-10 minutes

ACT Acceptance-Commitment Therapy

WHAT IT CAN HELP WITH
- Anxiety disorders

HOW TO DO IT

1 Lie down or just sit comfortably with your eyes closed.

Take a few deep breaths before you begin.

2 Observe your body.

Focus on high-tension areas like your neck and shoulders.

If you spend a lot of time at a computer, think of your lower back.

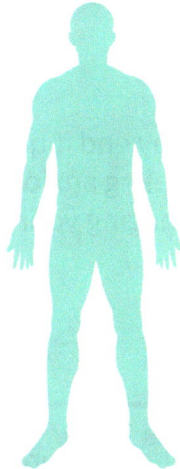

If you play sports, think of the body part you use.

Try to consciously relax these muscles.

3 Now think of a recent experience where you felt anxious.
Imagine the anxiety that you were feeling.

Think of its intensity,
the accompanying emotions, and the urges you felt.

You may become uncomfortable.
Just take deep breaths and stay with the emotion.

You will experience thoughts and judgments.

This is weird.

Let them come and go.

Do not engage.

Immerse yourself in the anxiety.
You are anxious, but you are safe.
This *will* pass, and it is only temporary.

Stay as long as you can with the emotion.
When you feel done, take a few deep breaths
and then open your eyes.

The first few times, you may end it quickly. But over time, you will develop a tolerance for feeling anxious. You will still feel anxious, but you'll be better at managing your thoughts, emotions, and behaviors.

WHEN TO DO IT
- When you are not anxious
- When you are in a safe place

CHAPTER 8
BEHAVIOR TOOLS

HABIT MANAGEMENT SKILLS

Emotions, thoughts, and physical sensations are automatically triggered by the fight-flight-freeze response. And while behavior is influenced by the urges that accompany the emotions, you have the power to resist them.

It's not easy, and it certainly isn't something you can learn to do overnight.

But it is possible.

There are three types of tools in this section:

- **Planning tools** that can help you plan your schedule better to avoid stress
- **Response tools** that involve consciously applying different behaviors in situations of anxiety
- **Anchoring tools** that help you ground yourself and feel safe

PLANNING TOOLS

Sometimes, we can anticipate anxiety from situations like an upcoming exam or a public performance.

Even something like moving to a new house is likely to cause a period of stress. Here are some tools you can use to manage your time better during these times and otherwise.

SMART GOALS

IN 1981 By George Doran, Arthur Miller, and James Cunningham

WHAT IT CAN HELP WITH

- Preventing stress

HOW TO DO IT

Sometimes we may set goals that raise our expectations too high, which can cause us undue stress and cause loops of irrational thinking.

I always mess up.

I'm just not good enough.

The next time you create a goal, make sure it is:

Specific, **M**easurable, **A**ttainable, **R**ealistic, and **T**imed.

SPECIFIC

A precise description of what you want to accomplish.

For example,

"Tomorrow, I'm going to study for the algebra test."

MEASURABLE

A limited portion that can be measured.

"I'm going to complete two chapters."

ATTAINABLE

Make sure you have the necessary means to complete the goal.

"I have some online resources that can help me understand the difficult equations."

REALISTIC

Set a goal that you can complete without aiming too high or too low.

"It takes me about an hour and a half to finish one chapter. So, I can confidently attempt two chapters."

TIMED

Set a deadline by which you want to accomplish the goal.

"I will finish studying by 6 p.m."

Setting SMART goals can help you plan your schedule better and prevent worrying about time.

WHEN TO DO IT

When you're making a schedule, a short-term plan, or a long-term plan.

POMODORO TECHNIQUE

DURATION As long as you need

LATE 1980s By Francesco Cirillo

WHAT IT CAN HELP WITH
- Time management

HOW TO DO IT

You will need a timer for this exercise. Make a list of tasks you need to complete.

1 Turn on the timer for 25 minutes and start working on the first task.

00:25:00

If you finish the task before the timer rings, spend the remaining time revising or doing a little extra.

2 When the timer rings, set the timer for 5 minutes and take a break.

00:05:00

Each cycle of working on the task for 25 minutes and taking a break for 5 minutes is called a pomodoro.

3 Complete four pomodoros before taking a long break for 15-20 minutes.

00:15:00

4 Make sure you tick off the tasks as and when you complete them.

1. Chapter 1
2. Chapter 2-3
3. Chapter 4

There are many reasons why the Pomodoro technique is a popular time-management tool:

- It breaks down large goals into small achievable tasks.
- The ticking of the tasks gives you a sense of accomplishment.
- The checklist gives you a visual idea of how much is remaining.
- It urges you to take a break, which is necessary to stay productive.
- The smaller duration of time to work is not as overwhelming.

WHEN TO DO IT

When you have a big chunk of things to complete. This can be studying for your exam or cleaning the house.

You can also use it to manage your time efficiently on any given day.

EISENHOWER MATRIX

DURATION 3-5 minutes

DWIGHT EISENHOWER 34th US President

WHAT IT CAN HELP WITH
- Time management

HOW TO DO IT

This tool is useful when you feel like you have too much to do and can't decide how to plan your tasks.

1 Draw four boxes with these labels:

Do it now.
IMPORTANT
URGENT

IMPORTANT
NOT URGENT
Do it later.

Delegate it to someone else.
URGENT
NOT IMPORTANT

NOT URGENT
NOT IMPORTANT
Don't bother.

2 Divide your tasks according to the label and make your to-do list accordingly.

For example, these are the tasks that you have:

- Study for chemistry exam
- Pick up a book for someone's birthday
- A pile of laundry
- Organize the family photographs

Your chemistry exam is coming up, and you need to study for it. So that is something you have to **do now.**

Your friend's birthday is soon, but you don't want to go pick up the book because you need to study, so **ask someone to pick it up for you.**

The laundry is crucial because you are close to running out of clean clothes. However, you have enough to last you a few days, so you can **do it later.**

You really want to organize the family photographs. It's been on your mind a lot, but it is something that you can do when you find the time. So, **don't bother.**

WHEN TO DO IT When you have too many things to do

WORRY TIME

DURATION 1-3 minutes

CBT Cognitive-behavioral therapy

WHAT IT CAN HELP WITH

- Stress management

HOW TO DO IT

Sometimes, you may be so worried that you have trouble thinking of anything but the source of the worry. In these situations, it helps to contain the worry to a specific time of the day.

> Set aside a time of the day where you will worry about what you are worried about.
>
> For example, you can decide to worry at 4 p.m. every day.
>
> If you have a worry that occurs at 6 p.m., you simply "park it" and deal with it during your next worry time.

This doesn't mean that you will instantly be free of worrying thoughts. It takes some time to get used to postponing worry, but practice helps.

WHEN TO DO IT

When you need to deal with genuine worry

ANCHORING TOOLS

These exercises are similar to grounding exercises, and you can do them to ground yourself quickly.

ON YOUR MARK

DURATION A minute

CBT Cognitive-behavioral therapy

WHAT IT CAN HELP WITH

- Situations that cause anxiety
- Anxiety disorders

HOW TO DO IT

1 Draw a symbol of your choosing on the space between your index finger and thumb.

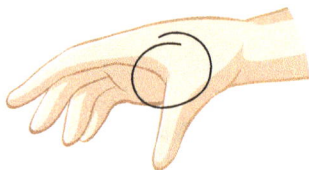

It could be a heart, a circle, an anchor, a bee, a robot, whatever you like.

2 Assign the drawing to a phrase or statement that comforts you.

Here are some examples:

- I am safe.
- It's going to be okay.
- I'm fine.
- Nothing is going to happen to me.

3 Every time you feel anxious, run your finger over the symbol and think of the phrase.

When you feel the association getting weaker, change the symbol.

WHEN TO DO IT   When you anticipate anxiety

ANCHOR TO YOUR SURROUNDINGS

DURATION | A minute

CBT | Cognitive-behavioral therapy

WHAT IT CAN HELP WITH
- Situations that cause anxiety
- Anxiety disorders

HOW TO DO IT

This exercise is similar to 'On Your Mark.' However, you need to anchor yourself to something in your surroundings rather than your body.

Decide beforehand what you're going to associate with the calming phrase or statement. It could be:

A tree

A mailbox

A doorway

Choose something you are likely to see in the situation you are preparing for.

Associating a doorway with safety can be particularly helpful for those with social anxiety. It can help you cope right before entering a room where you may have to meet people.

WHEN TO DO IT
During anxiety

ANCHOR TO YOUR PAST SELF

CBT | Cognitive-behavioral therapy

WHAT IT CAN HELP WITH

- Situations that cause anxiety
- Anxiety disorders

HOW TO DO IT

Set an alarm on your phone that will ring when you're likely to be in a situation that makes you anxious. Attach a note with a phrase that reassures you that you are safe.

You are safe.

Stop

When we're anxious, it is easier to have irrational thoughts. The purpose of the note is for rational you to assure irrational you that everything is and will be fine.

WHEN TO DO IT

When you anticipate anxiety

RESPONSE TOOLS

With any emotion, there is an urge to react a certain way. When we're angry, we may feel the urge to yell. But when we shout, we may make the situation worse. These tools are designed to help you respond instead of reacting, which can help slow down the anxiety.

OPPOSITE ACTION

DBT Dialectical behavior therapy

WHAT IT CAN HELP WITH

- Dealing with emotional urges

HOW TO DO IT

You know that feeling you get just before an oral exam, where you want to throw up or run away and hide? If you are having trouble calming down and focusing on your oral exam, this is a tool that may come in handy.

Opposite action is to do the exact opposite of what your emotions urge you to do. Here are some examples of opposite actions that you can do when you're afraid:

URGE	OPPOSITE ACTION	DETAILS
Get rid of the fear	Validate the fear	"Okay, I am feeling afraid."
Stay away	Confront	Approach what you fear
Stop	Continue	Continue what you're doing even though you're afraid

Run away or avoid it	Face the fear	Get it over with
Cower	Stand up to it	Stand tall; make yourself bigger; let your body reflect courage

WHEN TO DO IT   When faced with a non-threatening trigger

PROBLEM SOLVING

DURATION 3-5 minutes

DBT Dialectical behavior therapy

WHAT IT CAN HELP WITH

- Changing problematic behaviors

HOW TO DO IT

This tool is designed to help you change problematic behaviors. In the context of anxiety, this would include unhealthy coping behaviors, such as avoidance, negative self-talk, or substance use.

There are two parts to this exercise:

PART 1: INTROSPECTION

Choose an instance during which you used the problematic behavior.

- Describe the situation.
- What were the emotions you felt?
- What thoughts did you have?
- What did you do, and what were the consequences?

Now inspect it by digging deeper into the emotions and supporting thoughts.

List as many emotions as you can.

PART 2: MAKE PLAN B

Now think about the situation and see the different ways you could have dealt with things.

Using your list of emotions from part 1, list out the following:

- Emotion
- Coping thought
- Opposite action

Shortlist the best ideas and make a plan for the next time you are faced with the same trigger and the different ways in which you can respond.

WHEN TO DO IT   When you want to change unhealthy coping mechanisms

GRADED EXPOSURE

DURATION | 5-10 minutes to plan

CBT | Cognitive-behavioral therapy

WHAT IT CAN HELP WITH
- Anxiety disorders, especially phobias and social anxiety

HOW TO DO IT

The objective of this tool is to gradually increase your tolerance to situations and events that make you anxious.

1 Make a list of activities or situations that cause you anxiety.

Include different degrees of anxiety, from things that make you a little anxious to things that cause you to panic.

Making a plan   Taking a flight

You can also include safety and avoidance behaviors that you would like to stop doing.

Carrying a soft toy

Skipping social events

2 Rate them and arrange them in the order of least distressing to most distressing.

Start with the situation that ranks the lowest. Write down the trigger, the behavior with which you generally respond, and predict the levels of distress you will endure.

Rank	Trigger	Safety or avoidance behavior	Predicted distress	Actual distress
10	Making a plan	Avoid planning	4/10	
1	Taking a flight	Taking trains or not traveling at all	11/10	
5	Social events	Skipping them Making excuses not to go	7/10	
2	Leaving home without soft toy		10/10	

3   Complete the task and then rate your actual distress.

You may get nervous while doing this exercise, and that's okay. The exercise aims to become comfortable with doing the activity despite the anxiety. If you are unable to complete the task the first time, try again.

In time, you will be able to do the task without anxiety. Once you are confident with this activity, move on to the next one.

SELF SOOTHING

WHAT IT CAN HELP WITH

- Any level of anxiety

HOW TO DO IT

Soothing is the third type of grounding exercise. While you use your mind to do the exercise, it boils down to how you treat yourself.

Anxiety holds up a critical and exaggerated mirror to you. It brings up a dialogue that you would never imagine saying to another person.

Soothing is to consciously change the narrative of that dialogue every time it occurs.

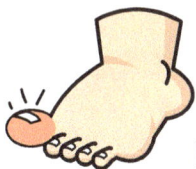

For example, you stub your toe and think, *Ugh, I'm such an idiot!*

Instead, you could think to yourself,

Oops, that was clumsy!

which removes the negative labeling.

To start with, observe how you talk to yourself.

Would you talk to somebody else this way? Are you being harsh on yourself? Are you calling yourself names? Are you being too judgmental? How can you rephrase the dialogue to be kinder to yourself?

Over time, your inner monologue will become calm and compassionate.

WHEN TO DO IT   Preferably, all the time

CHAPTER 9
TAKING CARE
OF EACH OTHER

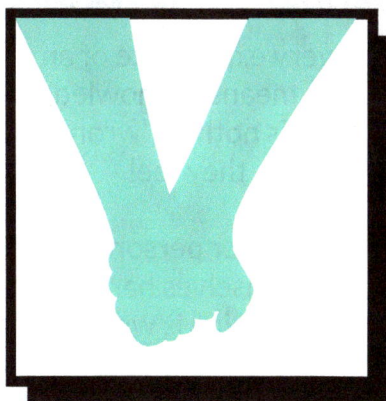

It can be challenging to relate to someone who has a hard time with anxiety. You may not understand what they're afraid of. You may want to help but not know how. You may unintentionally say the wrong thing. The best thing you can do to help is to create a safe space for them.

1

LISTEN WITHOUT JUDGMENT

A safe space is an environment where they can freely share their thoughts and emotions. When they talk to you about their anxieties or anything else about their life, listen to them without judgment. While it may be hard to do, resist the urge to give advice.

> **Do you wanna talk about it? I'm here to listen.**

2

VALIDATE THEIR EMOTIONS

Remember that every experience of anxiety is unique. To validate the emotion means acknowledging that they are in distress and that there is nothing 'wrong' with feeling the way they feel.

When we question another person's anxiety, they may feel excluded and judge themselves harshly. It may also work as an affirmation that something is wrong. This can escalate the anxiety and make them feel more helpless than they already do.

> **You seem very distressed.**

> **I can see that this is hard for you.**

2   LET THEM COME TO YOU

You may be in a rush to help your friend, but leave the ball in their court. Let them make the decision to share with you. Avoid asking too many questions and adding to the overwhelming nature of anxiety.

> You don't have to say anything if you don't want to. But if you ever need someone to talk to, I'm here for you.

OKAY, BUT WHAT DO I SAY EXACTLY?

The natural reaction to seeing someone trembling when you think there's nothing to fear is

> Uhhh... Dude, what are you doing?

But you're probably already aware that this is the least helpful thing you can say. Similarly, many statements made out of concern could actually backfire. They could make the person feel worse by causing an irrational thought.

Let's look at some common ones and the irrational thoughts they can trigger.

YOU SAY	THEY MAY THINK
What are you afraid of? There's nothing to be scared of.	*Oh my god, I'm going crazy.*
Maybe you should... (advice)	*I've tried everything. It's never going to get better.*
I don't think... (judgment)	*Nobody understands me.*
But you're so brave!	*I'm becoming weak.*
What's wrong with you? Why are you behaving like this?	*I'm broken; I'm damaged.*

Note: These two are especially futile because one person's stress doesn't reduce or remove another person's anxiety.

It can be more helpful to assure them that they will be fine and that you are there for them. If you're in doubt about what to say to make them feel better, it's best to simply say that.

OKAY, AND WHAT DO I DO EXACTLY?

It can be hard to decipher what to do when a friend is panicking or emotional because they're so stressed. Your instinct may be to ask them questions or to become anxious yourself. But this could fuel the anxiety and make it worse. Your friend is going through a natural thing, and they need you to remain calm.

- Be natural; continue doing what you're doing. Don't stare, and don't ask too many questions.

- Get them a glass of water.

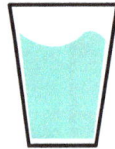

- Distract them with music or videos.

- Use a tool from this book.

- Remind them that they are safe and it will pass.

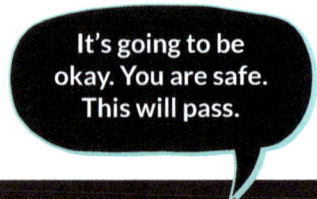

- Depending on your relationship, you can offer to hug them.

  > **Would you like a hug?**

- Let them know that they can ask you for anything they need.

  > **Let me know if you need anything.**

- Let them know that it is a safe space to share.

  > **This is a safe space. You can talk to me, I will not judge you.**

CHAPTER 10

RESOURCES

The World Wide Web is filled with helpful interactive resources for anxiety management. Here's a list of websites and apps that can help you use the tools in this book better.

	A smartphone app
	A website
	Adult guidance recommended

BREATHE2RELAX

Breathing exercises, body scan (pg 63)

CALM

Sleep guidance, meditation, breathing exercises

CALM.COM/BREATHE

A visual aid to help with deep breathing (pg 48)

APP.EISENHOWER.ME

An interactive Eisenhower Matrix tool (pg 138)

EXCELATLIFE.COM

Panic and anxiety assistance audios, and other resources

HEADSPACE

Panic and anxiety assistance audios, and other resources

JOURNALING TOOLS

Here's a list of secure online journaling tools:

- Journey.cloud
- Monkkee
- Penzu

MINDFUL.ORG

Mindful breathing (pg 51) and meditation (pg 114)

MOOD TRACKERS

Here's a list of highly rated mood tracking apps:

- Dailyo
- eMoods
- iMoodJournal
- MindShift
- MoodTrackDiary

NOTHING MUCH HAPPENS

Bedtime story podcast

POMOFOCUS.IO

An online customizable Pomodoro tool

TRACKS TO RELAX

A sleep meditation guide podcast

WORRYTREE

An interactive Worry Tree (pg 101)

In case of an emergency, you can reach out to

NATIONAL SUICIDE PREVENTION LIFELINE

📞 1-800-273-8255

🌐 www.suicidepreventionlifeline.org/

CRISIS TEXT LINE |

💬 Text HOME to 741741

🌐 www.crisistextline.org

THE TREVOR PROJECT

📞 (212) 695-8650

🌐 www.thetrevorproject.org

REFERENCES

The adolescent brain: Beyond raging hormones. (2011, March 7). Harvard Health. https:// www.health.harvard.edu/mind-and-mood/the-adolescent-brain-beyond-raging-hormones

Teenage sleep patterns. (n.d.). Michigan Medicine. Retrieved April 14, 2022, from https://www.uofmhealth.org/health-library/te7279#te7279-sec

Monroe, J. (2012, December 15). *Teenage hormones and sexuality.* Newport Academy. https://www.newportacademy.com/resources/empowering-teens/teenage-hormones-and-sexuality/

website, N. (n.d.). *Symptoms - Phobias.* Nhs.Uk. Retrieved April 14, 2022, from https://www.nhs.uk/mental-health/conditions/phobias/symptoms/

crufad.org. (2010). *Specific Phobias, Patient Treatment Manual.* St. Vincent's Hospital Sydney. https://crufad.org/wp-content/uploads/2017/01/crufad_SpecPhobmanual.pdf

Generalized anxiety disorder - Symptoms and causes. (2017, October 13). Mayo Clinic. https://www.mayoclinic.org/diseases-conditions/generalized-anxiety-disorder/symptoms-causes/syc-20360803

Najavits, L. (2002). *Seeking Safety: A Treatment Manual for PTSD and substance abuse.* Guilford Publications.

Bushra M,Ajaz A K. *Jacobson Muscle Relaxatation Technique (Jpmr) (20 Min).* JOJ Nurse Health Care. 2018; 8(1): 555726. 003 DOI: 10.19080/JOJNHC.2018.08.555726.

Journaling for mental health - health encyclopedia. (n.d.). University of Rochester Medical Center. Retrieved April 14, 2022, from https://www.urmc.rochester.edu/encyclopedia/content.aspx?ContentID=4552&ContentTypeID=1

CrashCourse. (2015). *The Nervous System, Part 1: Crash course A&P #8* [Video]. In YouTube. https://www.youtube.com/watch?v=qPix_X-9t7E

Polyvagal theory. (n.d.). Retrieved April 14, 2022, from https://www.rubyjowalker.com/polyvagal_theory.html

White, K. S., Brown, T. A., Somers, T. J., & Barlow, D. H. (2006). *Avoidance behavior in panic disorder: The moderating influence of perceived control.* Behaviour Research and Therapy, 44(1), 147–157. https://doi.org/10.1016/j.brat.2005.07.009

A SHORT MESSAGE FROM TEEN THRIVE

Hi there. We hope you enjoyed the book.

We would love to hear your thoughts on the book.

Many readers don't know how hard reviews are to come by,
and how much they help an author.

We would be incredibly grateful if you could take just 60 seconds to
write a short review on Amazon, even if it's just a sentence or two!

Log on to www.teen-thrive.com/review for instructions
on how to leave a review.

Thank you for taking the time to share your thoughts.
Every single review makes a difference to us.

www.ingramcontent.com/pod-product-compliance
Lightning Source LLC
Chambersburg PA
CBHW071942260326
41914CB00004B/720